YESTERDAYS

YESTERDAYS

by
LOUIS S. LEVY

LIBRARY PUBLISHERS
NEW YORK

"Act well your part; there all the honor lies."

Essay on Man, Alexander Pope
Epistle IV, line 194

DEDICATION

O Bounteous Nature, by whose arts
Thy sons were cast for divers parts,
Each to his task, his talents trained,
Rendered the offering thou ordained,
And passing, left a palimpsest
Of efforts well and truly pressed,
Let not the age that harvests all
Forget the toil which paid the toll.
But, hold in memory, fresh and clear,
Those heroes of the yesteryear.
Forgive their errors for their zeal
To raise the sum of common weal,
They were but human, not divine,
Their virtues, 'gainst their faults, align.
Each did his stint, as with his might,
Pursued his mission by his light.
Brave deeds, when smoke and dust have cleared,
Still be they cherished and revered!

TABLE OF CONTENTS

CONTENTS

LIST OF ILLUSTRATIONS

FOREWORD

These writings, not intended to be biographical, are but vignettes drawn from personal associations with certain outstanding figures of the recent past. As a partner of the late John B. Stanchfield, it was my privilege at close range to meet and to know these men who spoke freely of their history, their motives and their aspirations, thus revealing their techniques and traits of character. These recollections are presented not as my story, nor as a record of my personal activities, but merely as my impressions of these individuals resulting from the opportunity given me to learn at first hand about them, and to form my own estimates of them and their unique talents. The backgrounds, based largely on general knowledge, are presented merely as a setting for the individuals.

In his time each man was prominent in his field. Each had his problem and his opportunities. All were fired with high ambitions. What each accomplished and how he did it may reflect facets of his nature, illustrative both of the man and of his achievements. The pattern of their work may furnish an impetus for a new generation which knows them barely by name. If these episodes supply a bit of flesh and blood to great personalities now little more than a legend, they will have achieved their purpose. At least they should demonstrate that ours has been a land of boundless opportunity and unlimited privilege.

As the yesterdays quietly add themselves to history and the tomorrows emerge in rapid succession, the present is but an infinitesimal interval between them. The heroes of the past are too soon forgotten. We are so intent upon the future that we give scant attention even to the immediate past.

It is of course not possible from one's own experience to include all or many of the former outstanding leaders even of the immediate past. Yet these who are included present a stirring panorama in their respective fields of endeavor, significant, not only for its importance at the time, but also for its effect on their successors. Each was truly a master, an artist of his kind, making his mark and leaving an example, with a life story often stranger than fiction. Together they create a heartening picture of what wonders have been accomplished in America by real talent and sheer effort.

To each man was dedicated his objective. With some it was purely selfish, with others, there was an admixture of

generosity. Each was anxious to achieve this objective . . .
some regardless of the pain and suffering or sacrifice that
it might cause others and some always with human sympathy, careful not to hurt or damage anyone. In each instance, his technique was individual and original, but adapted,
as each thought, to serve his purpose.

There were those who found all-sufficient the prize they
sought, while others desired more, craving affection and
friendship. All courted and valued esteem, but not all were
willing to pay its price. In some there was a special talent
for friendship, while others appeared to disdain it, almost
to repel it. All enjoyed the thrill of battle, although they
differed widely in their understanding of its meaning and
in the use they made of it.

In these rather intimate studies of the individuals there
has been no conscious attempt to eulogize or to disparage.
Admiration for them is undisguised, for they were all leaders with distinctive and distinguished ability. It is hoped
that a glimpse at these great spirits as they chose to show
themselves, may serve as a challenge to high emprise as well
as a humble wreath on the monument of their careers.

YESTERDAYS

JOHN B. STANCHFIELD
(1854-1921)

My close association with John B. Stanchfield as
his intimate partner for more than a decade provided
countless opportunities for knowing the man such as
were given to no other person. While he was generally
inclined to be reticent and rather non-communicative,
he had no secrets from me. Without pride or apology,
he showed himself exactly as he was, sincere, frank,
and unreserved. In manner, address, as well as in
attire, he was the Chesterfield of the New York Bar.
A native of Elmira, New York, a graduate of Amherst
College, he first came into prominence as an outstanding baseball pitcher. All his life he was a baseball
"fan." It was said that while a student at college he
was the first person to pitch a curved ball, a feat
theretofore thought to be impossible. This was one
achievement of which he was proud. Before he was
admitted to the Bar, he was elected District Attorney.

He entered a prominent law office in his home
town, where he progressed to a partnership in which
his senior partner was David B. Hill, former Governor
of New York and later an eminent United States
Senator—one of the strong men of the Democratic
party who so strenuously opposed "Free Silver" and
its exponent, William Jennings Bryan. After serving
in the State Legislature, Mr. Stanchfield became a leading trial counsel, representing every railroad and every
large enterprise in his section of the state of New York.
He was called to New York City to act as trial counsel
in important cases, and in 1907 he located permanently
there, but still kept his Elmira office. For some four-
teen years, he constantly appeared as counsel to other
lawyers in trial and appeal courts, developing a dex-
terity in this work which won him universal recognition. He was frequently called to other cities because
of his outstanding ability as trial counsel.

In appearance he was most impressive: tall, handsome, well-groomed and suave. With his short-
cropped blond mustache, his dome-like forehead, pleas-
ing voice, and quiet, restrained manner, he emanated an
aura of respect and confidence. Extremely well-read
and scholarly, with an air of innate refinement, there
was no resisting the charm of this impressive man.
Never offensive or abusive, he invariably made a
friend of the Court, of the jurors, and even of his

opposing counsel. As he was neither elated nor cast down under any circumstances, it was impossible to detect either his pleasure or his disappointment in the progress of his cases.

Mr. Stanchfield had no pride of opinion in the preparation of his cases. He would gladly receive and fairly consider any suggestions from the humblest member of his staff, and indeed would be eager to get them. He would often ask his associates to prepare a line of cross-examination, which, while he might not use any part of it, would be lodged in his mind for future reference. He had unshakable confidence in their work. His implicit faith lay in preparation.

Until he was fully prepared, he could not be induced or forced to go into a trial. Then he would have a strategic plan based on his theory of the law and the facts, sharpened by his keen insight into human nature, reinforced by his charm of manner and his cogency of address, with which he could always register. His cross-examination was quiet and courteous even with the most hostile witness. He had none of the leonine ferocity of Samuel Untermyer, nor the serpentine adroitness of Max Steuer. He would never ask a question when he felt unsure of the answer. His presentation was as cleverly put together as an edifice, so that he rarely met with a surprise. While he could rise to oratorical heights, he preferred to deliver a re-

strained, conversational address, sensing the effect as
he went along. All courts paid him great courtesy and
deference, for they trusted him. However they might
be obliged to decide, they could not avoid the desire
to yield to his great personality. They liked to see him
win. Accordingly, this man, so restrained and so considerate, in his own quiet way, soon had a score of
victories of which every lawyer stood in awe. When
any prominent attorney found himself in personal difficulty, he would seek out Mr. Stanchfield in whom he
always found a sympathetic and sagacious counsel;
and for such services there would be no compensation.

It was in a long drawn-out case that he showed to
best advantage. The better acquainted he became with
the Court and jury, the stronger was his personal appeal. Moreover, he would study his opponent's case
as carefully as his own. While his arguments had
force as well as clarity, it was all in the spirit of fair
play, without resort to recrimination or personality.

Mr. Stanchfield's dry humor was shown in an argument on a statutory law wherein Felix Frankfurter,
later a United States Supreme Court Justice, appeared
in opposition, making a learned and ingenious presentation, full of intricate and fine distinctions. Rising
to reply, Mr. Stanchfield said merely: "I have been
intrigued and educated by the learned 'mosaics' of my
opponent, but the liberty of a client does not depend

on such tenuous casuistry." In a phrase, he had aptly and completely frustrated the effect of a very telling argument, although it cost him some misgivings to cast a reflection on one for whom he had sincere respect. This was the only instance in which he indulged in a seeming personality, but here he could hardly be criticized, for this was the only answer he was able to make.

Often his opponents, exasperated by his calmness and courtesy, would deliberately attempt to involve him in a personal squabble, but always without success. Nothing and no one could disturb that imperturbable serenity. Juries came to think that one so self-possessed and so confident, so well-prepared and so fair, could not be wrong. Many a client he won from out of the jury box. Important men of affairs deemed it a privilege to confer with him. When he came into a case as counsel to other lawyers he would never belittle them or attempt to monopolize the limelight. Their suggestions would be welcome, although the ultimate decision would be his. He would not shrink from any duty which he was called upon to perform; he would go into a police court as readily as into the United States Supreme Court, and he would treat the police magistrate with the same deference as he would show the United States Chief Justice.

John Stanchfield was essentially a modest man. He

perfect. He made it plain that the accountant did not mean to lose his record this time. Then he asked whether he realized the iniquity of presenting a false statement to the Court and jury. At once the accountant was on the defensive. He said that he would never be a party to such injustice. He declared that he would vouch for every figure in every schedule he presented; that he had checked and rechecked each one; and that he would stake not only his reputation but his whole testimony on the accuracy of each figure.

Mr. Stanchfield then said: "Let us see. Please go to the blackboard and write thereon a column of figures which I shall read to you. You yourself and the Court and each juror as well as my friends of the prosecution may verify them as I read them." Taking up the particular schedule, he proceeded slowly to read off the figures. When he had finished, he asked whether he had read them all correctly. There was no demur by any one of the many who were closely following his recital. Then he said: "You realize that this column is most important to the issues of this case, don't you?"

"Yes," was the response, "I know its great importance."

"Then," said Mr. Stanchfield, "kindly add up the total on the blackboard. Take plenty of time. Let us see how accurate you are. We shall each of us add up the figures for ourselves and compare our results.

Perhaps some of us may be quite as accurate as you are."

The witness slowly made his addition, and his total was $1,000,000 more than the total of the schedule. Comparing the two, he saw the mistake. After vainly striving by repeated attempts at a rectification, he turned, crestfallen, to his questioner and said, "I must admit that I made a mistake of *one* in the total on the schedule."

"One?" asked Mr. Stanchfield in a voice of thunder. "You mean one million, don't you?"

"Yes," conceded the witness, "the *one* in the million-dollar column."

"Do you deny that your schedule is wrong to the extent of one million dollars in showing the credit balance of this defendant on the day in question?"

"No," came the answer, "it was an inadvertent mistake for which I am very sorry."

No further comment was needed. Court, jurors, and attorneys alike, thrust the schedules angrily aside with visible disgust. Thus did Mr. Stanchfield dispose of those devastating schedules. From that time on no one mentioned them again.

In the wake of his victories he left no enemies. His favorite indulgence was to meet a choice few of his lawyer friends at a good dinner. There they would indulge in pleasantries and yarns and moderately im-

bibe Irish whisky or Rhine wines. Their golf perfor-
mances were a favorite theme for discussion. One of
Mr. Stanchfield's amusing golf stories had to do with
Judge Morgan J. O'Brien who was his constant opponent at golf. One Sunday after a game, the Stanchfield chauffeur was taking Judge O'Brien home when
the Judge for a lark said: "Mike, how do you like
your job with Mr. Stanchfield?"

"Fine," said the chauffeur.

"Does he pay you regularly?" asked the Judge.

"He certainly does," answered the chauffeur, "and
he says he always will, so long as he can play golf
with you."

*   *   *   *

Politics would be barred in his meetings with his
lawyer friends; also their own cases, except when they
would twit one another about what appeared in the
press.

Mr. Stanchfield once confessed that despite his long
experience and his familiarity with the courts and
cases, he never opened a trial or an argument without
stage-fright, but from which he speedily recovered.
Whenever he had argued an appeal, he was disturbed
if the Court or any of its members complimented him
on his argument. Greatly as he relied on his associates

he preferred to have none of them accompany him to court. Strangest of all, after he had finished a hard case, he would refrain from discussing it. Neither did he wish to be questioned about it, even when he won. He would never talk about his cases. Often he would come back to his office and ask for a memorandum of law. When given it, he would accept it without question and rely upon it absolutely.

Praise of his work made him uncomfortable. Whatever others might think of him as the arch advocate, it was clearly apparent that he himself had no exaggerated ideas of his own importance. But this did not make him pessimistic. He was always a heartening comforter to those in trouble. No matter what the case, if he undertook it, he put his whole heart into it, and became so sympathetic that he always believed his cause just, even when it might appear hopeless; not that he underestimated the difficulties, but to the end that his presentation carried the clear implication of sincerity and honesty.

In the selection of a jury, he was patient and painstaking, forming quick judgment on the talesmen from their appearance. In a famous criminal case in which he was defending an important man whom he had decided not to place on the stand—a difficult procedure which he often successfully pursued—the jury box was filled, but two additional talesmen had been called, to the latter of whom he was immediately attracted. He was a Mr. Fitzpatrick, a bright, clear-faced Irishman, who held a position of trust. "That is just the kind of man I would like to have on the jury," he whispered to me. But how to get him was the question, as he had no more peremptory challenges, although the prosecution still had one. So he quietly proceeded to re-examine the jury, and contrived to get one man to express a suggestion of prejudice and another to indicate a disposition to favor him. On his application to the court, the first was excused for cause, and the District Attorney promptly challenged the second. So Mr. Stanchfield's choice became number twelve in the jury box.

During the course of the long trial, juror number twelve was so deeply interested that he kept making notes in a little black book. By no look or smile did he show any sign of favor to the defense. When the prosecutor finished his summation, Mr. Stanchfield was annoyed to see that number twelve seemed to clap his hands. Turning to me, Mr. Stanchfield whispered: "Well, I need not have gone to all that trouble to get number twelve." The jurors went out and after an interval came back to the jury box. In passing Mr. Stanchfield, number twelve winked at him with a faint smile. The verdict was "Not guilty."

A few moments later, lawyers, jurors, and witnesses

went over to the old Astor House Bar for some re-
freshment. Number twelve came up to Mr. Stanchfield, and said: "Governor" (as he was popularly
called) "that was a magnificent performance of yours.
There was never a time in the trial when you had not
won."

"Thank you," was the hearty reply. "But tell me,
my dear fellow, didn't I see you applaud the District
Attorney when he finished?"

"You may have," answered number twelve. "I was
so damned glad he was finished that I may have un-
consciously clapped my hands."

* * * *

So often was Mr. Stanchfield retained in difficult
cases that it became almost a by-word that the case must
be hard, if not hopeless, because it went to him. Realizing that this was a dangerous handicap, he took the
greatest pains to demonstrate that he was actuated by
his own convictions rather than by a professional obligation. He never allowed a case to run itself. Always
he had a plan and an objective from which he seldom
deviated, and the plan was usually so sound and effective that it required no changes. Perhaps this was the
reason why he was looked upon as the cleverest strategist at the bar. But to one who had the opportunity to
know him well, his greatest talent was not his tech-

nique, superb as that was, but the pervasive charm of
his personality. This was the secret of his success in
his long, complicated cases. Surely it was not due to
flights of oratory, in which, though capable, he would
seldom indulge, nor was it due to the bludgeoning or
snaring of witnesses, nor to courtroom artifice, nor to
personal exchanges between counsel. When he talked
to his jurors, he neither spoke down to them nor affected to descend to their levels. As man to man he ad-
dressed them, in clear, simple, well-chosen phrases,
catching and holding their interest, and inducing a
sympathetic reaction while tactfully directing their
reasoning powers.

Mr. Stanchfield's courteous attitude was never more
effective than in a case in Washington, D. C., where
prominent bank officials were on trial for certain reports which the Government claimed to be untrue. It
was a case in which much adverse local feeling had
been aroused; there was great enough inaccuracy in
the reports — though unintentional — to induce Mr.
Stanchfield to keep the defendants from the stand. The
only defense was "a reasonable doubt." To bolster
this defense, he called to the stand a portly, kindly
gentleman who gave his name as William H. Taft,
testified that he had been a Federal Judge, Governor
of the Philippines and Cuba, Secretary of War, President of the United States, and was now a law lecturer

at Yale. Former-President Taft soberly testified to the high character and good standing of the defendants. He was excused without further questioning and quietly left the courtroom.

Suddenly a loud noise was heard outside. People rushed to the windows. Marching down the street was a great cheering crowd led by "Teddy" Roosevelt, who soon burst into the courtroom, shook all the counsel by hand, bowed to the court, and promptly seated himself in the witness box. After the usual questions as to his public services, Mr. Stanchfield asked: "Colonel Roosevelt, when you were President of the United States, did you or any member of your family keep a deposit in the bank of these defendants?" Before an answer could be made, the prosecution interposed an objection which was sustained on the ground that this was not the proper way to introduce character evidence. Thereupon Mr. Stanchfield asked: "While you were President did you know the character and reputation of these gentlemen in this city?"

Quick as a flash Roosevelt shot out his answer: "Yes, Mr. Stanchfield, it was so good that I and every member of my family kept an account with their bank!" Then, showing his teeth in a broad smile, he glanced toward the jury. When he was excused, he whispered to the Judge, who nodded. The Colonel walked over and shook hands with each juror.

Mr. Stanchfield had been told that the Judge would be so hostile that he must impress this upon the jury by constantly fighting the Judge. Quite the contrary. He was all courtesy and consideration toward the court. In his summation he dwelt only upon the "reasonable doubt" arising from the "'character" evidence, explaining the intricate decisions and their application with great detail and patience—to such effect that the court in its charge to the jury complimented him on his courtesy, his clearness, and his accuracy, saying that nothing should be added or subtracted from Mr. Stanchfield's fine presentation of the effect of character evidence. There was a prompt acquittal. The Judge invited Mr. Stanchfield into his chambers. He complimented him on his conduct of the trial, saying it had been a privilege to be there, then said: "I just want to say one thing to you, Mr. Stanchfield: it pays to be a gentleman!"

Mr. Stanchfield would have graced any bar at any period. Although he was never assertive in any public movement, he had a splendid legislative record, had been a worthy candidate for governor though defeated by the first Odell landslide, and was mentioned for the Senate in the protracted party contest which finally selected O'Gorman. He was always glad to give his aid to any meritorious public effort. His activity in the elevation of Benjamin N. Cardozo was such an instance. Some four times Mr. Stanchfield had been drafted by the Democratic party of New York City to do an outstanding but unpleasant job. The last time it was to take charge of the impeachment proceedings against Governor William Sulzer. Without any compensation, he performed that distasteful duty which elevated Lieutenant Governor Martin Glynn to the governorship. Some months thereafter, when he was discussing the gratitude of Governor Glynn with me, I said: "I suppose Governor Glynn would like to do something worthwhile for you."

"Yes," responded Mr. Stanchfield, "I believe he would. But what do I want?"

"You may not want anything personally, but you could do a great service to the state," I suggested.

"What service have you in mind?" he answered.

"Well," was the reply, "there is a very good lawyer in this town who is but little known. He has one of the greatest minds in the country. He is extremely modest and self-effacing. I know him well and admire him intensely. He has written a standard treatise on the jurisdiction of the Court of Appeals. He has just been narrowly elected as a Judge of the Supreme Court. He does not belong on the lowest court, but on the highest."

"If you really think so," said Mr. Stanchfield, "get him over here and let me talk to him."

Cardozo was sent for, was told of the suggestion, and said that it was his dearest ambition to sit on the Court of Appeals, but that he had no hope whatever of getting there.

Mr. Stanchfield then asked Cardozo to prepare a resume of his past activities, and said that he would be happy to explore the situation. Cardozo expressed his appreciation and promptly delivered about a half sheet of typewritten data. Mr. Stanchfield told me that this was too fragmentary, and delegated me to elaborate on it. When this was done, he first made sure that he could spell the name correctly and said he would take it up with the Governor. Soon after he reported that the Governor was deeply interested in what he told him about Cardozo, but had halfway promised the appointment to another.

Thereupon Mr. Stanchfield said, "Governor, your candidate is an excellent man, but mine is an outstanding man. If you appoint mine, you will be remembered for that appointment when everything else you have done is forgotten."

"Well," responded the Governor, "if you think as highly of him as that, I shall certainly reconsider."

Not long thereafter the Governor had sent for Mr. Stanchfield and said: "Mr. Stanchfield, I am very grateful to you for your suggestion. I find that your man— what's his name?—is most highly regarded by the

Court of Appeals. They need two men there. Now if
you will get William B. Hornblower to accept, who
has twice declined my offer, I will appoint him and
your man at once. By the way, please write out his
name for me."

While this was pleasant news, it placed Mr. Stanchfield in a very embarrassing position. At the time when
he was a partner of David B. Hill, the latter, as a
Senator from New York, was having some difficulty
with President Cleveland, who was determined to
make an appointment to the United States Supreme
Court without consulting the New York senators.
Twice the President attempted to do this, unsuccess-
fully, once with Wheeler H. Peckham and once with
William B. Hornblower; then, yielding to the senatorial custom, he appointed Peckham's brother, Judge
Rufus B. Peckham, who was duly confirmed. Therefore Mr. Stanchfield feared that as the former partner
of Senator Hill who had frustrated Hornblower's elevation to the United States Supreme Court he would
be an unfortunate emissary from Governor Glynn to
induce him to accept a place on the New York Court
of Appeals. However, he went to see Hornblower. He
came back with an acceptance on the condition that
the appointment and confirmation by the State Senate
should take place on the same day, as Hornblower did
not wish to be subjected to partisan criticism for his

long and devoted service to the large corporations.

As several weeks had elapsed since his interview with Cardozo, Mr. Stanchfield told me he must have an unqualified acceptance from him before he reported to the Governor. Post-haste, I rushed up to Judge Cardozo, and interrupted him in the midst of trial. "Judge, I am only a messenger sent on a special errand. I cannot give you any assurances or make any promises. Mr. Stanchfield wishes me to get your unqualified acceptance of a Court of Appeals appointment, if the Governor decides to appoint you."

Cardozo replied, "You did not need to ask me. I told you some time ago how I felt about it. Of course I shall be most happy to accept. I cannot quite believe it is true."

To this I replied: "I think it is really true and I am inclined to believe that it will take place today." I then hurried back to Mr. Stanchfield, who telephoned the Governor at once. That afternoon the two gentlemen were duly appointed.

Cardozo started on his remarkable judicial career, which led to his unanimous election as Chief Judge of the Court of Appeals and later to his appointment by President Hoover as a Justice of the United States Supreme Court. Mr. Stanchfield's prophecy to Governor Glynn was realized—this was the outstanding act of his administration.

Judge Cardozo, who died in service, everywhere came to be regarded as one of the outstanding judicial minds of the century. It may be of interest to note that in Mr. Stanchfield's first case before the Court of Appeals after Cardozo's accession, that Court was divided three to three, after which Judge Cardozo cast the deciding vote against him. Mr. Stanchfield frequently referred to this as a tribute to Judge Cardozo's courage and integrity.

This incident was but one of many such in Mr. Stanchfield's career. He was frequently consulted by those in power as to the capability and fitness of candidates; and always his advice was unselfish and sincere. One occasion gave him great personal pleasure— when his old associate and partner in his Elmira firm, Frederick Collin, was nominated by both parties and elected to the Court of Appeals.

One of the outstanding cases which Mr. Stanchfield handled was the murder trial of Harry K. Thaw.

His office was besieged with requests for passes to hear the case, but one close friend of Mr. and Mrs. Stanchfield showed no interest in the case at all, and though asked several times whether she would like to attend, she steadfastly refused, giving as her reason her lack of sympathy with the case. In fact, she was disappointed because Mr. Stanchfield had taken the case, inasmuch as she was convinced that Thaw was not a

man who should be allowed his liberty because of
his erratic behavior.

On the day of the summation this lady came to my
office a few minutes before noon, and as I was too
busy to offer her lunch, I suggested she go to the courthouse where she would find Mrs. Stanchfield, who
would lunch with her.

"Definitely not," she replied. "You know how
strongly I feel about the case."

"But," I demurred, "it is only a few minutes before
twelve and court adjourns at noon, so you won't have
any time to listen to the case."

She finally consented, and I sent one of the young
men from the office to show her the way.

The crowd around the courthouse, shoving and strug-
gling to get in, was so great that they were literally
compelled to fight their way through.

It seemed paradoxical that hundreds of people were
attempting to get in without avail, whereas this woman,
who had no desire to enter, could do so.

However, they finally managed to reach the courtroom and the lady quietly seated herself. Her eyes
happened to light upon a rather distraught-looking,
disheveled, red-haired man with popping eyes, and her
conviction as to Thaw became stronger than ever.

In a very few minutes the Judge announced a recess
for lunch.

Immediately my friend found Mrs. Stanchfield. Mrs. Stanchfield said that Mr. Stanchfield would join them in a few minutes and they would all have lunch together.

As soon as they were seated at the luncheon table Mr. Stanchfield turned to the lady and said, "How did you happen to come to court, since you disapprove so strongly to my taking the case?"

To which the lady replied, "I was in town for the day, and I was told your wife was in court and might lunch with me, but," she added, "I haven't changed my mind about Thaw. Anyone looking at him could see he isn't normal."

"Which one did you think was Thaw?" asked Mr. Stanchfield.

"The third man from the end, of course. No one could mistake him."

"Oh," said Mr. Stanchfield with a broad grin, "that wasn't Thaw, that was the district attorney," and he burst out laughing.

Then he turned to Mrs. Stanchfield and said, "Clara, how would you like to meet Thaw? He's dining in the next room with a guard."

She replied, "Yes, I should like very much to meet him."

Mr. Stanchfield thereupon wrote a note and gave it to a waiter to take to Thaw in the adjoining room.

Shortly thereafter Mr. Thaw came to our table.

The lady stared in surprise at this good-looking, well-spoken man, who greeted her so courteously.

He remained to chat for only a few minutes and then returned to the adjoining room.

Then Mr. Stanchfield invited the friend to return to court with them.

Having been completely won over by Thaw's manner, she decided to do so. She listened to Mr. Stanchfield's masterly summation and then the jury filed out.

Thaw's mother, who was sitting directly in back of the lady, leaned over to Mrs. Stanchfield, and with tears streaming down her face, said, "Whatever the verdict, Mrs. Stanchfield, I want you to know how grateful I am to Mr. Stanchfield for his kindness and sympathy and wonderful understanding."

Mrs. Stanchfield put her arms around Mrs. Thaw and burst into tears.

The lady who did not want to attend the trial at all sobbed louder than anyone else.

*   *   *   *

Mr. Stanchfield contrived to get much enjoyment from his professional contacts. One of the ablest and sternest judges in the Federal Courts of New York was Charles M. Hough, a man of fine literary tastes, an extremely profound lawyer, a cool, austere judge, but a man of deep feeling, despite his detached manner, with a remarkable but dry sense of humor. While Judge Hough overawed most practitioners because he would tolerate no nonsense, ineptitude, or indirection, Mr. Stanchfield always looked forward with pleasure to an appearance before him. They became social friends who delighted in each other's company, yet face to face in court they were almost total strangers. Once in a most important trial Mr. Stanchfield questioned a witness, asking "Whether or no" a certain man careless of finances left a substantial fortune. A strange thing then happened. Down came Judge Hough's gavel. "Counsel will please try to use good English in this Court," was the judicial utterance.

Quietly and undisturbed, Mr. Stanchfield turned to the Judge and speaking for the record in low but audible tones: "May it please the Court, for whom I hold the highest respect, in matters of English language, I hope that I may be pardoned for holding some few others in even higher respect."

"Who, for instance?" demanded the Judge. "Produce your authority."

"Professor Thomas Lounsbury of Yale," answered Mr. Stanchfield.

The spectators, curious as to who the victor of this unique combat would be, awaited the Judge's reply.

"The Court will give you just one week to produce Professor Lounsbury's opinion," ruled the Court.

Within one week, Mr. Stanchfield laid before the Court Professor Lounsbury's approval of the phrase as accepted usage, and Judge Hough at once placed in the record the Lounsbury opinion with his own apology.

In another case when it came to Mr. Stanchfield's summation before Judge Hough and a jury, he noticed at recess that Mrs. Hough was in the back of the courtroom. After he had finished, he greeted her cordially and courteously, asking why she had come.

"Well," she replied, "the Judge told me that if I wished to hear the address of a lifetime I should come here to hear you. I came, and I was not disappointed."

Notwithstanding this sincere friendship, Mr. Stanchfield never asked a favor or a privilege from Judge Hough. He had a habitual phrase which he frequently employed: "I will never ask a man to do anything for me which I would hesitate to do for him, if he were asking me." His tolerance with difficult and obstreperous lawyers was amazing. They were like terriers trying to antagonize a great dane. When his associates would object or complain, he would say: "Don't be too critical. You might do the same if you were in his place."

After Stanchfield's untimely death in 1921, at the age of sixty-seven, Senator Root, consoling me, said, "I have seen many great trial lawyers in my day; in fact,

I think I have seen them all, but I have never seen his equal in a courtroom. I doubt whether there have been many like him."

Francis L. Wellman, often a redoubtable opponent of Mr. Stanchfield, in his famous book, *The Art of Cross-Examination* (page 194), says:

"Mr. Stanchfield combined the qualities which make a great advocate. Tall in stature, very erect, with great depth of chest and breadth of shoulder, a large and shapely head, and a handsome countenance, his presence was commanding. His voice was strong and resonant, and his speech evinced an unusual command of pure and simple English, perhaps the result of his fondness for reading the classics. He had the power of clear and concise statement, whether of fact or law, a fine imagination, a keen sense of humor, a mastery of irony. And when the occasion required, he was capable of eloquence of a high order. In the trial of cases he was alert and resourceful, and never became disturbed or confused, even when the unexpected took place. Indeed, his composure under all circumstances and his courage in the most desperate crises were the chief weapons at his command. He was a past master of the art of cross-examination, always respectful to the Court, and so fair in presenting his case in attacking his opponents that it is not surprising that juries gave him verdicts. His ability, industry, and loyalty to his clients go without saying and were universally recognized; but the memory of his overwhelming courtesy and politeness to everyone he associated with, in and out of court—clients, judges, jurors, witnesses as well— will long remain in the minds of everyone who knew and loved him."

In his last illness, when he realized that he was beyond relief, I had a last touching interview with him. Propped up in bed, with his high color making him look as strong and handsome as ever, he heard the death sentence unmistakably pronounced by his friend Dr. Joseph Blake. A tear started to roll down his face, the last thing one would expect from this strong, undemonstrative man. Then he said: "This is a fight I shall lose and very soon."

"No," I ventured, "you have won many tougher ones, and you will win this one. Nobody can look as well as you do and be as sick as you think."

"I know better," he said. "I know all about this chronic nephritis. But I have had a full life and I have enjoyed every moment of it. You look out for my wife and family. They will be safe with you. But I have one great regret."

"What is that?" I asked him.

"Leaving you," he answered, and then he proceeded to dictate a memorandum of unfinished matters which he wished to be attended to. That done, he held out his hand, and with a wan smile on his face, he said, "Good-by, God bless you. Go down to Mrs. Stanchfield and do what you can to help her."

During his last years, when he felt his fatal illness gradually progressing, expressions of personal affection appeared in his letters to me, the more remarkable for one who was always rather repressed, not given to emotional demonstation. In 1918, at the beginning of his illness, he wrote:

"I appreciate the personal note of affection that runs through your letters, and believe me, they are reciprocated. I should feel like retiring if anything went wrong with you."

Within one year of his death he wrote: "You would make as great a success, if you were to take up litera-ture, as you do in the law. I cannot pay you a higher compliment.

"What I could not say to the stenographer—a new one to me—is that my association with you, profes-sional and personal, is the happiest and pleasantest of my life. Your kind and anxious solicitude for my wel-fare under any and all circumstances will never be forgotten. Your regard for me has begotten a love for you that time cannot change. Always to the end, Yours faithfully, John B. Stanchfield."

In another of his letters he wrote: "You have be-come closer to me than a son."

On his passing a flood of tributes poured in from all over the nation. A few excerpts from letters of some of the leaders of the Bar who have since passed on, and who well knew how to choose their language, may reflect their measure of this outstanding personality.

Senator Edgar T. Brackett, often his opponent, and once his colleague (in the Sulzer impeachment) wrote: "The profession is infinitely poorer for his passing. I am one of those who believe that he stood in the very front rank and well toward if not the head of his calling, not only in state but in nation, and he must be ranked among the great lawyers of the world."

William D. Guthrie, more often his adversary than his colleague, wrote: "Stanchfield leaves a memory of splendid talents, of great professional distinction, of high regard, of warm, admiring and devoted friends. He was a lawyer of great talents and a man of exceptionally attractive and lovable qualities."

George L. Ingraham, former Presiding Justice of the New York City Appellate Division, before whom he had argued many cases, wrote: "He was one of my oldest friends and for the last five years I have become very close to him and have learned to love him so much that it seems like the death of a brother."

So ended the spendid career of one who, though his life was spent in battles, left no enemies; who, though careless of finances, left a substantial fortune;

with the face of a sphinx, had a heart of gold, and whose passing was an occasion for mourning and tribute in all the courts in which he had exercised his outstanding talents. The Bar has lost an ornament, his friends have lost a loyal, inspiring companion, and the world has lost a great and good man. He was a true gentleman in his manners, a fine scholar in his tastes, and a real artist in his work.

SAMUEL UNTERMYER
(1858-1940)

Among the outstanding barristers of the immediate past none was more remarkable than Samuel Untermyer, the paramount dialectician of his time.

With a ferret-like mind and a mentality undaunted by any complexity, he had the rare faculty of mastering every situation of the many which he studied, and then of pressing his points to the utmost, regardless of their effect on the feeling of his adversary or of the unfortunate whom he was questioning. No opponent gave him pause. Savage and unrelenting in cross-examination, so keen and resourceful that nothing escaped or eluded him, he was a born prosecutor, brilliant, hard, and merciless. His withering sarcasm knew no restraint.

Opposition merely redoubled his energy. His favorite activity was to rush into some great reorganization or into a financial debacle, and there to wield his battle-ax right and left, sparing nobody and omitting nothing. As counsel for the Federal Pujo Committee of Congress, he did more to uncover financial unsoundness and irregularity in high places than had ever been done by any other advocate since the Hughes Insurance Investigation. It was this work of his which brought about the major changes in financial regulations and unrestrictive operations of the country, and which gave rise to the Federal Reserve System, in the formation of which he had a major participation. The greater the personage, the more eager he was to test out his motives and his objectives.

As counsel to the Lockwood Committee he tore the heart out of iniquitous labor and building conditions in New York, bringing about many great reforms. To him nothing was sacrosanct once he found an irregularity. In his work he was a veritable czar. Nothing could distract him once he started. In a committee investigation Untermyer was supreme, if not omnipotent; as prosecutor, Court, and jury, he tried the issues in his own fashion, he made the rulings conform to his wishes, and he wrote the verdict as he chose. The Committee became merely a stage-setting for him as the star performer.

His mind was encyclopedic. He could absorb his facts with lightning rapidity. When he had shattered an outstanding figure or a great institution, he was quick and resourceful in picking up the pieces.

In the process of rebuilding he would be keen to participate. Such participation proved most profitable to him in amassing a private fortune. He was always a reformer, but he was likewise a careful, farseeing businessman and a most able accountant. His fortune, probably greater than that of any other practitioner of his time, grew largely out of the various situations which he handled. Starting with a brewery combine with English capital, he emerged as a very large investor in mining companies, steel companies, railway companies, oil companies, publishing companies, mercantile companies, and even movable food trailers, commonly called "street diners"—all of which made money for him. All were carefully watched by him.

Untermyer had the reputation of charging large fees for the cases he tried, and there is an amusing story about a carpenter he represented who had fallen from a roof and was badly injured. Many months after Untermyer had begun suit, he wrote the carpenter that he had won the case, but that it was being appealed. After the lapse of several months, Untermyer informed the carpenter that he had won the case in the Court of Appeals but his opponents were bringing the case before the Supreme Court and he would notify him of the result when the verdict was rendered. Finally, after the passing of many more months, Untermyer wrote

the carpenter that he was glad to tell him he had won
the case and he was enclosing a bill for $5,000. His
client replied that he was happy to learn of Mr.
Untermyer's victory, but he would like to ask just one
question, "Who fell off the roof, you or I?"

Untermyer was adamant as to his charges. No lawyer was more astute as to what a given situation would
yield, nor more effective in securing it. Lawyers and
clients realized that while his services were not to be
had cheaply, still he gave full value for what he received. Busy as he was, he would neglect his lucrative
practice to do a public service. Woodrow Wilson as
President, and "Al" Smith as Governor, both frequently requisitioned his assistance. He worked closely
and effectively with Senators Glass and Owen in cur-
rency and financial reforms. All this was without pay.

When World War I started he came in for some
public criticism, as he had previously been socially intimate with many of the German representatives here.
But no act or statement of his could be fairly called
unpatriotic. Long before World War II he led a
nationwide crusade against religious persecutions im-
posed by the Hitler regime, and there was no greater
Hitler antagonist in America. He foresaw the terrible
cataclysm which was imminent, and he contributed
all his power and resources to avert and to combat it.

His grasp of a subject was phenomenal, whether it

be manufacturing, mining, machinery, finance, or balance sheets. He would get directly to the heart of the matter. He could then assemble his material with infallible accuracy, missing no innuendo or insinuation in emphasizing or garnishing it. No one was a more effective master of invective, no one more blistering in attack. His arch enemies would end up by being his friends, for there was no withstanding the power of this extraordinary, dynamic individual. He compelled respect by virtue of his achievements, and no one was especially anxious to invite his opposition.

The remarkable feature of his activity was the variety of his efforts. He undertook every sort of litigation. A specialist in corporate law and financial problems, he would suddenly appear in a hotly contested marital squabble. From unraveling the Kruger-Toll debacle, he would rush into the Stokes divorce case. The Stokes case became a memorable event. Pitted against each other were two redoubtable opponents, Untermyer and Steuer. The issues of the case gave way to a personal conflict between counsel. Untermyer, with all his driving power and preternatural shrewdness, a veteran of numberless successes, met a younger man in his full maturity who was a specialist in just such an action. Untermyer did not have all the odds in his favor here. Stomping on like a raging lion, with furious invective, he would attempt to deliver

his crashing blows only to find that his wily opponent
had cleverly dodged them, and, like a swaying cobra,
had implanted a stinging fang in the onrushing foe.

It was like a duel between gladiators, the one with
a broad-sword, the other with a rapier. Conscious of
having been baffled, and smarting from the sting,
again and again Untermyer would crash head-on,
only to be eluded and to suffer more stings. But the
stings were not enough to stop him. Bitterness, incri-
mination, vituperation, and violent personalities flew
back and forth. The Court found it difficult to separate the contestants in their clinches. The tide of battle
fluctuated from day to day, even from moment to
moment. A simple lawsuit had become a vicious personal battle between two champions in forensic pugil-
ism. Their mutual detestation was unconcealed, due
more to their mutual realization of frustration than to
actual animosity. Neither, with all his verbal resources,
could find language severe enough to characterize his
opponent. Each might wound the other but neither
could secure a "knockout." Unfortunately neither
achieved a victory in that hearing, for the Court retired
before a decision, and the case disappeared into that
limbo where it had always belonged. Its only outstanding feature was its battling advocates. It has been
said that Untermyer ultimately prevailed for the wife.

From then on each of these skilled advocates con-

ceived a wholesome respect for the other, and each
had a sincere appreciation of the other's ability. They
did not become friends, but they were no longer enemies. Steuer knew that in Untermyer's proper sphere
he could not be beaten; Untermyer knew that on
Steuer's special stage Steuer was incomparable. Undoubtedly each envied the other for something which,
while he recognized it, he could not emulate.

Untermyer had the knack of keeping himself always in the public eye. With all his acrimonious controversies, deep down he had a heart, even though in
the thick of the fight it seemed to disappear. He always played a "lone hand" which, despite his monumental achievements, did not always win wide publicity for him.

His one great hobby was flowers. He knew the
English and botanical names for every kind and species, and guarded each bloom as a treasure. His hothouses were a vision to behold; in them he also raised
exotic fruits. One Sunday when he had invited his
friends, Morgan J. O'Brien and John B. Stanchfield,
to lunch, they came rather late after their game of
golf. They told Mrs. Untermyer that the reason for
their tardiness was because they had stopped at the
hothouses, and had liberally partaken of the Untermyer nectarines. She begged them not to tell Untermyer of their raid on his precious fruit. She said he

kept a strict guard on his nectarines, as they cost several dollars apiece. As to this, Judge O'Brien promised secrecy, inasmuch as he said they had consumed many more than they could count. The fact was that it was only a "joke."

In his day no one made so many great enemies or brought about so many needed reforms. All in all, Untermyer was, in his way, a genius, without a peer in his work. Judged by his outstanding results, he richly earned the respect and gratitude of the vast public for whose benefits he labored so hard. William Guthrie, who was generally on the side of his wealthy opponents, he angered and humiliated by his savage attacks, but in the end these two held each other in high respect, with a regard akin to affection. Guthrie had a refinement and a scholarly aloofness which Mr. Untermyer looked upon with awe. Untermyer had a tiger's brain and a lion's courage which Guthrie could not but admire.

While Untermyer appreciated friends, yet he did not make many among his co-practitioners. He seemed to shrink from friendship as though he thought that it might hamper him by restricting his freedom of activity. On one memorable occasion he gave me unmistakable proof of his friendship. It was while he was counsel for the Lockwood Committee and was attacking a proposed combination of five of the most important independent steel companies. I was selected to make a personal protest to him and to show him that such a merger would benefit, not harm, the building conditions. Called on the telephone for an appointment, Untermyer snapped back: "What do you wish to see me about? If it's about your steel merger, you can save yourself the trouble. You should not use our friendship for a business advantage."

"Well," I replied, "I shall not answer your question. I did not think that your friends had to present an agenda in order to see you."

"Oh, forget it," he answered. "Come up to Greystone for dinner."

"No," I said. "After what you have said, I prefer not to dine with you. Yet I will come up at nine o'clock to see you. Please remember that I will not ask you to do anything you ought not to do." I found him greatly dejected and visibly unhappy.

"I'm disgusted!" he moaned. "Here I am doing voluntarily a public service without pay, with everybody, including all the newspapers, against me! The more decent the work I do, the more enemies I make."

Such conversation went on for a least an hour, until he seemed to have gotten over his dejection. There was no mention of the steel merger, directly or indirectly. Then without prelude, he announced: "I know that you wish me to drop my attack on the steel merger.

Well, I have thought it over carefully and I now believe that the merger might be a good thing for the industry. Tomorrow morning I shall say so publicly."

Despite this intense partisanship he had been able to see the other side and had reached what he believed to be a fair and impartial judgment. Friendship may have softened his attitude, but it was a sense of justice and fair dealing which determined his course.

Acquisitive as he was by nature, he would be generous once persuaded as to the merit of an appeal. But he was besieged by so many appeals that in self-defense he was obliged to erect an effective barrier from those who constantly sought a personal conference. Removed from the arena of battle, no one could be more sympathetic or understanding. He was known for his liberal contributions to civic and philanthropic organizations irrespective of race, creed or color. Letters from all over the country were received daily and he would contribute after careful investigation, but he disliked to be asked solely on the basis of a personal relationship. An amusing story is told of a woman whose friendship he valued highly who wrote to him for a substantial contribution to a charity in which she was deeply interested. Receiving no reply, she sent a second note reminding him of the desire he had expressed to be of service should she ever need advice or assistance. She wrote that she was now availing her-

self of that offer and would be grateful to him if he
would plead her case with one Samuel Untermyer.
Her reply was a number of invitations to luncheon
at Greystone, which she ignored.

They met one evening at a dinner party given in
honor of Untermyer's departure on an extended Euro-
pean trip. After greeting her cordially, he asked why
she had declined his invitions. He told her he had been
deeply grieved by her neglect and wanted to know the
reason. "The reason...." she replied, "you know the
reason very well, Mr. Untermyer. In fact, I would
rather not have come to this dinner given to wish you
a *bon voyage* had I not been coerced into coming. I'm
not interested in the kind of voyage you have."

He smiled broadly as he said, "Oh, I suppose you're
cross with me because I didn't answer your appeal
for a donation to your charity? He laughingly added,
"If I give you whatever I have in my wallet, will you
make peace with me and wish me a good trip?" Believing that he would certainly have a few hundred
dollars, she agreed. Untermyer counted out five hundred dollars. Handing over the money, and shaking
his finger at her he said, "Remember, young lady, this
is a special gift and don't ask me for it again next year.
Now you can wish me *bon voyage* and, since you have
cleaned out my pockets, you can give me carfare to
take me home."

"With pleasure," was the answer. "I'll do better than that. I'll take you home myself in a taxi and I will be glad to wish you the best of all voyages. And, in spite of what he said, he sent a generous contribution yearly, unsolicited. Difficult as he habitually made it for his friends and even for his family, his devotion to them was deep and generous. Yet in the closest of his relationships, a sharp difference of opinion or a spirited argument was ever in the offing, as he was prone to a contentiousness which not even he could repress; and this he often regretted.

In an era of great advocates, Samuel Untermyer must be placed with the topmost. He mastered every problem which confronted him. He met the leaders of the American Bar in deadly combat and generally carried off the victory. A great accountant, a brilliant barrister, a resourceful industrialist, a phenomenal financier, he shone pre-eminently in every activity to which he devoted his marvelous mentality. If all his activities be considered, though others might be found of equal ability in special lines, their combination left him without a peer in his time. He was in truth a consummate artist, a veritable genuis in his work, and withal, as Mr. Stanchfield once said, a "thorough-bred."

MAX D. STEUER
(1871-1941)

Max D. Steuer was an Austrian Jew, the son of poor immigrants. From a lowly clerk he rose to be one of the greatest of cross-examiners. He would begin in an almost inaudible voice to force close attention. Then, in a prepared crescendo, his voice would grow first shrill then harsh. He did not claim to be a profound student of the law, though he never was at a loss for the precedents which he needed, and few could employ them as effectively when necessary. He was not an appeal lawyer, for in that chastened atmosphere he had not the opportunity for the full play of his special abilities.

Steuer's place was in the trial court before a jury. Only there did he have ample range for his operations. His accurate knowledge of human nature, his ability to evaluate the reactions of the average man who sat on his jury, offered him the proper scope for

his talents. He hardly needed to look at the jury to
know just how each member was disposed. He had
a sure instinct for the vulnerability of a witness. It
might be on a most immaterial point, but to that spot
he would drive, elaborating that weakness to such a
degree that it seemed to be the turning point in the
case. In listening to any story, he could at once seize
upon its strength as well as its weakness. The strength
of his case he would emphasize, the weakness he
would protect.

While his summations were strong and convincing,
they were merely a smashing recapitulation of the
points made in his grilling examinations. From the
very inception of the case he was making his summation. By his cross-examination he usually impaled a
hostile witness on the horns of a dilemma. Extracting some clear-cut admission from him by a series of
simple questions, step by step he would lead him
into an inextricable morass. Then to burnish the point,
he would go back to the basic admission, giving the
witness the opportnuity to amend his statement. From
this new statement he would lead him unerringly into new and even more hopeless entanglements. The
witness would be not only cornered but hopelessly
lost. No juror could fail to perceive the destruction.

With an infallible memory for testimony and figures,
he would cautiously await an occasion when his op-

ponent made a misstatement, however inadvertently. Upon this he would pounce like a mountain lion, and proceed ruthlessly and literally to tear him apart. Unless he was sure of his ground, he would not make the attempt. But it was disastrous to enter any dispute with him in a courtroom as to figures or as to a bit of testimony which had been previously given. If Steuer threw down the gage of battle, the victory was inevitably his. Without a note or a paper, he carried every line of the most voluminous testimony on the tip of his tongue, and that tongue was blistering and shattering. Likewise, gifted with a rare aptitude for figures, he not only mastered them in a trice, but always had them ready for immediate use.

Sometimes he would confront a trial judge, who, knowing his tactics and his proclivities, would attempt to frustrate them. Then he would not hesitate to turn on the Judge, to impress the jury that he was being hurt by adverse prejudice or unfairness. Close to the line of contempt he frequently went, but always he kept just on the safe side, so that while the court was nettled and angered, he could not administer judicial castigation. There were greater lawyers, cleverer strategists, more learned students, than he, but no other man more tellingly effective before twelve jurors, whether the Judge was with him or against him.

His specialty was close "in-fighting" with his opponent. There was no ruse or twist in a "give-and-take" exchange of a trial with which he was not familiar, or which he disdained to utilize when he thought it effective. Never exuberant in victory, he was always dejected in defeat. No one, not even he himself, could foresee the precise progress of his cases. Frequently he would win solely by his courtroom tactics when he had little other ammunition. But he had the disheartening habit of discouraging his clients by pessimistic forecasts. While the jury was deliberating in a great case which he knew he had already won, he would be apt to say that it was lost, as in the Mitchell case. But a case had to be hopeless indeed and a trial bare of any fortuitous incident for him to lose it. While at his best in cases involving personal relations or matters of conflicting evidence, he made no distinction in the cases he would undertake. As a successful trier of criminal cases he had no superior. No one excelled him in resourcefulness and performance in a criminal court.

To many it seemed that Steuer suffered from an inferiority complex. It may have been this which inspired him to do his utmost on every occasion. Deep down he had a reverence for the leaders of the bar. After so many years it pained him to realize that he did not enjoy that respect in which he secretly held them. Openly he would be disposed to belittle them. But

when at last his outstanding ability was recognized
by high and low alike, his attitude changed entirely.
He became more careful about his choice of causes,
happier in the company of his fellow lawyers, and less
caustic in his criticisms.

His attitude toward clients was unusual. Many attorneys, some the greatest, feel it a personal tribute
to be chosen by a client. Steuer soon outgrew this
feeling, if he ever had it. He believed that clients
came to him for what they could not get elsewhere;
and so his terms were inflexible, immutable, and even
might appear to have been exorbitant. It was a case of
"take it or leave it." His acceptance of a retainer he
treated as a privilege extended to the client.

In one of the most important cases of his career,
when he had been chosen, somewhat reluctantly, to defend a very prominent individual, he flatly refused to
appear in court until every cent of his fee had been
paid to him in advance, although he knew that victory
in that case would mean more, as it proved, to raise
his professional standing than any other case in his
whole career. He would not allow this opportunity
or this tribute to his skill to interfere with the value
which he placed upon his services. It is indeed doubtful whether another such instance can be found in the
history of great advocates.

I once brought him a case involving a man named

Charles Mitchell the president of National City Bank.

The stock of the National City Bank had taken a terrific drop and Mitchell was being indicted by some of the stockholders.

Mitchell had retained as counsel General Wild Bill Donovan, assistant district attorney under Herbert Hoover and later head of the secret service. I called on Mr. Mitchell to discuss his case.

Mitchell said: "I want to ask your opinion; I want you to sit and listen to my case, and tell me what you think I ought to do."

When he got through, I said: "Mr. Mitchell, you want a frank statement, don't you? I think you have a complete defense, but I must tell you I think you will be convicted."

"How is that possible?"

I said: "I'll tell you. The feeling against you in New York is so great, so many people lost money in your stocks, no matter what you do, you're licked before you start."

"Is that America?"

"Yes, that's America. It's the hue and cry of the people who have lost money."

"You think I am innocent?"

"I do."

"Have you any suggestions?"

"If Mr. Stanchfield were alive, he could save you."

"Is there no other man in this great country?"

"There is another man. There is only one man, in my opinion, who is capable of undertaking your case. He isn't popular, he won't have your respect, you won't like him, everybody will think you are guilty the minute you retain him, but he might prove you innocent. His name is Steuer. He is the only man to-day capable of trying a great criminal case."

"Everybody will think I am surely guilty. I'd be ashamed to tell my lawyers."

"I'll tell them," I offered.

All his lawyers had the same reaction. I said: "You are all able lawyers, but you don't know a thing about it. This man is an expert. If you had a severe operation, you would select a man not for his looks, but for his skill."

I was delegated to talk to Steuer. "I have come to offer you the greatest case of your life. You have been practising law in this town a long time. You have no respect for the top-level attorneys, and the same can be said of them toward you. No one has ever appreciated you and ranked you as you should be, and that is what has hurt you. Now I come from the leaders of the bar to bring you the case they can't handle, and they concede you are their superior."

"Whose case is it?"

"Charlie Mitchell."

Steuer demanded $100,000 cash before he would go into court. Mitchell said he couldn't raise it. He had $50,000, but Steuer refused to go into court until he had the balance. Two days before the case came to court I laid the other $50,000 on Steuer's desk.

From the opening of the case Steuer kept telling Mitchell that his case was lost. It was his technique. When the jury went out, he said: "I'm sorry, but it will come in 'guilty.' " In about half an hour they came in "not guilty."

From then on every National City case went to Steuer; it changed his business but not his nature. He still remained the perennial egoist.

About a year later Steuer came to me and said: "I have an extra check for my services. It's yours. You never got any money for your work on my case."

*   *   *   *

Steuer finally overcame all his handicaps—his personal unimpressiveness, his discourtesy to clients, to lawyers, and even to courts (though never to juries), his abiding sense of injury, his conviction that he was frowned upon and considered alien by the elite, and his lack of that intangible something which wins friends. At the close of his career he no longer needed to overdo himself in registering his high abilities; no longer did he feel oppressed and excluded. After one

or two great cases which he affected to accept unwill-
ingly from the recognized leaders, he was finally regarded by them as truly a master in his field. Yet with
all his ability, he lacked the leavening sense of humor.
Neither did he have the high privilege of acquaintance
with the literary, artistic, or historical great. The soft-
ness and the elegance of a cultured background had
never been accorded him. No man more admired the
gentle graces nor craved them more dearly. They
would have spared him many a painful moment and
many a heartache. All the greater is the victory which
he won without them. While he could rise to thrilling
heights in developing pity and compassion, these were
not his natural traits. He was a specialist in swaying
the mind and heart of jurors in his own peculiar way.
He ranks high in the roll of great barristers of his
time because of this outstanding talent before the
twelve men in a jury box.

In his work he was merciless. He neither gave nor
expected any quarter. With him there was no friendship in business. In action he was as bitter toward a
friend as he was toward an enemy. But his instincts
were so shrewd that they seemed almost infallible.
Unbounded sarcasm and destructive insinuation were
his favorite weapons of attack. He appeared to know
just how to reach and sway the ordinary mentality, and
seldom was he mistaken. His cases were always close

and difficult. Indeed, it was generally thought that it must be a hard or well-nigh hopeless case if it went to him. But even this did not appear to affect the score of his victories. It was said that while another prominent lawyer might be thought in advance likely to win, only to turn out unsuccessful, Steuer, with a supposedly losing case, would emerge the winner.

During the John F. Curry administration in Tammany Hall, Steuer became a political power in the city, for he was generally regarded as Curry's principal adviser. When any of "the faithful" landed in difficulty, they turned to Steuer for advice. But his influence did not sway Governor Roosevelt, and despite all his efforts to save Mayor Walker, he worked in vain. It was he who handled the Bank of the United States debacle. He was appointed as Special Prosecutor, and as such he personally conducted the complicated Grand Jury proceedings, brought about the indictments, and himself convicted the bank officials. Then he did his utmost to convict the State Superintendent of Banks of negligence, who was appointed and supported by Governor Roosevelt, but in this he failed.

Some of his cases were truly remarkable for his courtroom achievements. In the defense of the Triangle fire case, involving the death of more than four hundred girls who perished in a fire trap, he suspected that a young woman who was the most dangerous witness against his clients had learned her story by rote. Cautiously he led her into several repetitions of parts of her story by which he plainly demonstrated this to be the fact, thus demolishing her evidence and thereby acquitting his clients.

In the prosecution of Gardner, one Foelker, a former State Senator, told a damning story about Gardner attempting to bribe him to vote against the Hughes Anti-Racing bills. Foelker was the Senator who, carried in on a stretcher, cast the decisive vote in favor of the Anti-Racing bills. Cautiously, Steuer questioned him about his early history, forcing him finally to admit that he had hired a poor student to take his Regent's Examination for the Bar and had thus "passed" in subjects as to which he was obliged to confess his total ignorance.

When Foelker, plainly cracking up, was released from the witness box during a recess, he rushed from the courtroom, disappeared from sight, and was never heard of again. Thus Steuer won two sensational cases in which it seemed that he did not have even the faintest hope of success. The public had become so furiously aroused that the defendants stood already convicted; a trial appeared to be a useless formality. These victories were regarded as phenomenal.

Like many men of outstanding ability, Steuer was a composite of varying moods and of uncertain temper.

From these the chief sufferer was himself. Still, he had the comforting faculty of proving satisfactorily, at least to himself, the correctness of all his views and all his actions. Having known the privations of poverty, he was determined to acquire wealth. Having suffered the disdain of his fellow practitioners, he was eager to win their respect. Both of these objectives he attained and in a high degree. But at what cost in suffering and effort was known to none but himself.

He was a most interesting conversationalist, but he was never more interesting than when he talked of himself, a subject which he would discuss most thrillingly and without urging. Yet one forgot the egoist in the charm of his story. It was a story close to his heart, in which he could place the highlights, the colors and the shadows, with the skill of an artist. One never tired of that artistry in which he generously indulged. With his unique endowments and a personality neither impressive nor engaging, he "pulled himself up by his bootstraps," achieving a recognized eminence among his fellows, reluctantly but finally accorded, and nonetheless conceded by his enemies who were indeed more numerous than his friends. That he was a great practitioner none could deny. Having won that distinction, with the emoluments which it brought, he seemed to care for little else. In any trial which he undertook he proved himself a savior for his client but a demon for his opponents, to whom his very appearance was a danger signal.

He was always a devoted husband and a kind, fond father. Indeed, he had great qualities; but magnanimity and tolerance toward adversaries were not among them. He had neither the erudition nor the isolation of the abstract scholar. With him a legal battle was a war in which the only objective was to win. The motive by which he was impelled and the ends which he sought, justified, in his judgment, all his methods and all his tactics. His adversaries were constantly agonized and frequently embittered. He always played a lone hand with little thought or care for the feelings of those whom he fought.

His sole personal indulgence in his leisure seemed to lie in the excitement of a gambler. He rather fancied himself as a bridge player, and, while he disdained the set rules, he still developed considerable expertness. He also took a keen interest in the theater, owing perhaps to the fact that for years he had been very active in theatrical controversies. But, despite his wide and varied acquaintanceship, and his knowledge of human nature, his friendships were but rarely deeply emotional. He was, in truth, a most unusual person, who during his life had received few favors and seemed rather inclined to measure those he gave by those he received. As a trial counsel in jury cases, he fully earned his exigent fees, for he was a specialist who had in his time and in his special arena no superior and few peers. Of course, he did not win all his cases; for, as was once said by a great English barrister, the only advocate who wins all his cases is the one who does not have many.

DE LANCEY NICOLL
(1854-1931)

De Lancey Nicoll was a gentleman to his fingertips. He represented, socially, the "top drawer." Descendant of a pre-Revolutionary, well-to-do family of Dutch descent, with a name always prominent in New York, he was a man of great refinement, excellent education, wide experience, a keen wit, and an irrepressible sense of humor. His firm, soon after his appointment as District Attorney, rose to a rank which was shared by not more than a half-dozen others.

He was a skillful advocate who had served his apprenticeship in the rough and tumble of trials, and he missed no opening for advantage. He knew the force of satire and the deadly effect of reducing his adversary's argument to an absurdity. His trials were always enjoyed by both Court and jury, although not by his opponents. He could quickly detect the strength and the weakness in a case, could argue profoundly when necessary, and could elaborate the highlights effectively and convincingly. Few other lawyers could more accurately appraise an opponent.

While not studious, he employed excellent research men who kept him constantly supplied with ammunition which he knew so well how to use. There was no one more alert to the exigencies or opportunities of a trial, and no one who could turn a quip or ring the changes more effectively. He worked hard and he played hard, without ever losing his smile or his good humor. An able, resourceful advocate, he had at his command all the qualities of a skilled trial lawyer.

In conjunction with this remarkable acumen as a trial lawyer he possessed the knack of popularizing himself under all circumstances. Without undue friction or pride of caste, he went along, always doing a good job, never worried or distracted, satisfied when he had done his duty. He had the faculty of "sizing up" his fellowmen with startling keenness. He could answer a long, tiresome argument in one pithy, humorous phrase. He could describe an individual in a few sharp words with all the suggestive power of a Rembrandt etching. But he had no patience with pretense or trickery; no tolerance for the tawdry or the cheap. Though a purist, he was occasionally Horatian and sometimes Rabelaisian in verbiage.

In his time Nicoll handled very successfully many

large and important matters. His mentor was his able assistant and research authority, John D. Lindsay. Unexcelled as was Lindsay's ability, it would have been fruitless were it not for the manner in which it was employed by Nicoll. The latter was of a time when lawyers rode the circuits, when frolicsome diversion had its effective place in work; when the courtroom was a stage for the display of forensic ability, quick thinking, sharp repartee, and personal magnetism. In all of these he was adept.

Between Mr. Stanchfield and Nicoll was mutual respect with mutual admiration and deep affection. When opposed, it was like a spirited match of thoroughbred boxers, Nicoll always having his joke, Stanchfield unruffled but steadily pursuing and registering his point. But when they were together they presented a remarkable exhibition of power and humor.

For all his raillery, Nicoll was an ingenious tactician. His opponents could ill afford to be off guard even for an instant. He never forgot what he was after and he usually obtained it.

Nicoll loved life and he reveled in the pleasures of living. Fortunately he was able to gratify himself to the fullest extent because of his means and his position. There was neither overindulgence nor profligacy in his nature.

Inclined to sacrifice solemnity to humor, quick to

scent the opportunity for sarcasm, he never missed a
chance to create an effect; but his manners were always impeccable and his objectives justifiable. After
a long, hard day, fighting vigorously with a worthy
opponent, he and his adversary would often leave
the scene of combat arm in arm and repair to some
neutral spot, there to spend the evening in delightful
badinage and camaraderie, without a suggestion of
animosity. Next day the battle would be resumed. For
Nicoll work was a thing apart, but good fellowship
always in order.

This rare good fellowship often stood him in good
stead. In the sharp hostilities engendered by the Government's suit to break up the great Tobacco Trust,
Nicoll had a major part for the defense. When the
Government was victorious, the public expected a
disastrous dismemberment of this financial colossus.
But Nicoll went to work on the order for the judicial
execution. By his suavity of approach and his pervasive fairness, he brought about a decree which, while
it carried out the court's decision, involved the minimum of damage to the arch industrialists whose fortunes were affected. From the viewpoint of a personal
achievement, it is doubtful whether this record has
ever been equalled.

Stanchfield and Nicoll failed in the two outstanding
cases on which they worked together. One was the

defense of attorney Abraham Hummel, who was prosecuted for his part in the notorious Morse divorce case.
They had deep-seated respect for the talents of this
man, with a feeling bordering on affection. They defended him without fee, and although they put their
hearts into it they could not save him.

The other was the famous Reader case. Reader was
suing J. B. Haggin for a commission on Haggin's purchase of the great Cerro da Pasco copper mine. The
case came originally to Nicoll. He induced Mr. Stanchfield to try it. Their adversary was Francis L. Wellman. True to type, he brought off a devastating coup
by suddenly springing some damaging letters. Mr.
Stanchfield was obliged to terminate the trial on the
grounds of surprise. The plantiff threatened a damage
suit unless the case were tried again, and this time
without a fee. Mr. Stanchfield, after fully explaining
to the client the futility of another trial, reluctantly
agreed to retry it. He did the best of which he was
capable, only to meet with defeat before his learned
friend Justice Dowling. But this time even the obdur-
ate plaintiff was convinced of the hopelessness of the
case. The letters could not be denied; their explanation did not win credence.

The last case Mr. Stanchfield argued against Nicoll
was the Stillman divorce case. Bitter as was this contest in the courts, cautiously and aggressively as each

of these trial experts watched each other for an opening, sharp as were their attacks and counter-attacks,
there was never even a shade of antagonism in their
personal relations. Yet, neither gave nor asked quarter.

It is such a spirit as Nicoll's which brings zest and
joy into professional life. Never malicious, always gay,
his was the philosophy of the smile in the routine of
work. His wit was devastating but it had no sting.
He was indeed an ornament to the Bar, a tower of
strength to his clients, and a fountain of good will
and good cheer to his friends. His friends were legion,
his opponents many, but his enemies none.

Nicoll was a very able lawyer, a fine performer,
a master technician, universally conceded to be highly
skilled in his job, and, above all, he was a perfection-
ist, who proved that a successful advocate need never
cease to be a true gentleman.

FRANCIS L. WELLMAN
(1854-1942)

Francis Wellman had been Assistant District Attorney under De Lancey Nicoll. Then it was that he first displayed his wonderful skill as a trial lawyer in the most difficult criminal cases. In the notorious murder trials of Carlyle Harris and Dr. Buchanan, he constructed an irrefutable arraignment of facts, made up, like a mosaic, entirely of numberless bits of evidence, which the defense had omitted to notice. When all these were fitted together with his diabolical ingenuity, they formed such a compelling picture that it proved that the defendants had in truth woven their own halter.

Wellman was the first man to send a victim to the electric chair, and always regretted that he had to do so.

He had a perfect court manner. He was quiet, respectful, and precise in his presentation, particularly careful and fair though searching in his examination of talesmen for his jury, which he deemed an important function. As an expert on the complicated rules of evidence, his cross-examinations were models of clarity, simplicity and objective. But there was drama in all that he did. He understood the advantage of climax, of suspense, as well as of surprise. Step by step the witness would be led where Wellman had predetermined. If, then, he could maneuver to spring a surprise, the effect would be catastrophic. And so his opponent had not only to know his case well, but had to be eternally vigilant to ward off an unlooked for flank attack.

A case which involved chemistry, psychology, or any branch of science was his metier. As an insanity expert he had no superior, and as a detective in ferreting out crime, and in putting together the bits of evidence into an array which became overwhelming, he surpassed the most fertile writers of detective fiction.

Wellman was well-bred and well-educated, with a mind as sharp as a razor. He could use it either as a sledge-hammer or a rapier. As an authority on the art of cross-examination he wrote a treatise, *The Art of Cross-Examination,* which has become a textbook. For the leaders in that work he always had sincere respect, and an accurate estimate of their abilities.

Frequently did he cross swords with these leaders, always with credit to himself, whatever the result. He wrote four other textbooks: *Days in Court, Gentlemen of the Jury, Luck and Opportunity,* and *Success in Court.* Each of these is a splendid exposition of the consummate practice of law before Judges and juries, and each regales tales of great lawyers, great Judges, and great trials of the past. No other man has better expounded the technique and the effective conduct of the trial of cases before Judge and jury.

He was a master of surprise. Ceaselessly hunting for some unusual point in the evidence, he would proceed very cautiously, first to win the confidence of his witness, and then to lead him to the block, where the ax would fall with unerring aim. Frequently he reversed the tide of the battle by some startling development which no one had suspected. Another of his clever tactics was to induce a witness to repeat certain excerpts of his story, and then to confront him with the divergence in the telling, magnifying the difference until a trivial variation seemed to have become the most vital factor in the case.

Wellman was distinctly a trial advocate, who spent his whole life in courtrooms. He was but little interested in other phases of practice. In the company of other great barristers he felt most at ease, and to them he brought much from his knowledge of the world, with his keen understanding of human nature. He had many sharp, bitter fights with Untermyer and yet he had a real affection for him. Toward Steuer, while perhaps he did not have affection, he had esteem for those abilities which he so accurately rated.

Wellman outlived many of his cherished companions but he never forgot them, and as long as he lived he enjoyed reminiscing about them. While a redoubtable opponent and a resourceful adversary in the arena of battle, yet he was always at heart sincere, and always a generous opponent. Assuredly he belongs in the first category of the great barristers of an era noted for its leaders.

His familiarity with literature was such that it was dangerous even for the most erudite opponent to garnish an argument or to adorn a point with a quotation. Almost in a twinkling he would retort with a phrase or a line which would demolish without leaving a trace. He was not only effective; he was also thrillingly interesting; not because of eloquence such as Littleton's or of power such as Untermyer's, nor of cunning such as Steuer's; but because of the sheer logic of his argument and the unanswerable force of his point. As a finished trial counsel, he was ready for any emergency.

Each case presented two problems which must be completely solved before he would go into a trial;

first, the problem of preparation; second, that of generalship in its presentation. With him, a trial resembled a military engagement, involving strategy, emphasis, protection, surprise, attack, logistics and finally, reserves.

For many years Wellman was the leading defense attorney in damage suits brought against the street railway companies. No one was better informed on all the twists and turns of the law, nor more successful. Likewise he was adept in defending insurance cases, of which he had many. In criminal cases, the field in which he had his early training, he was more effective as a prosecutor than as counsel for the defense. Yet in that series of prosecutions in which New York City Police Inspectors were tried on graft charges, his client was the only defendant who escaped.

Wellman's greatest forte was in matrimonial litigation. Here he was able to stir the emotions, usually successfully, in proving his client the victim, not the offender. His conspicuous faculty was his psychological keenness. In this respect he much resembled Steuer as a "tiger brain." No less familiar than Steuer with the devices and ruses in a jury trial, each found a worthy antagonist in the other.

On one occasion, growing out of a fierce matrimonial controversy, he seemed to have detected Steuer's subtle hand in the evasion of a grand jury subpoena.

So he went after him remorselessly. But when further investigation exonerated Steuer, no one could have been more prompt in its acknowledgement than Wellman. The situation arose from any attempt by a former wife to reach a fund set aside for her benefit which was to be forfeited in the event of her annoying her former spouse. It was claimed that she had mailed to him a scurrilous letter. Wellman contended that this forfeited her interest; Steuer denied her authorship and maintained that her rights were unimpaired. After a spirited fight which went through all the courts, replete with aggressive rancor, Wellman won, but the fight left scars on each of the combatants. In the course of this fight Steuer narrowly extricated himself by his personal appearance before a Grand Jury which alone saved him from indictment.

Despite their many sharp clashes, when Wellman came to write his splendid book on the leaders of the Bar, he gave an important place to Steuer.

In those two early famous capital cases, the Harris and the Buchanan, Wellman had to fight formidable adversaries. His work here was a marvel of skillful, patient examination and masterful presentation. It won for him nation-wide admiration. Both cases involved the knowledge of toxic drugs and intricate therapeutics. It was in just such situations that he appeared to greatest advantage. From these two cases he rose at once to the highest rank of prosecutors. Gratified as he was by these successes, and without a shade of doubt as to the guilt of the defendants, he frequently expressed a personal regret that he had been the instrument which sent them to their doom.

Wellman was distinctly opposed to litigation, except as a last resort. Frequently he declared that a poor settlement was better than any victory, and he always did his utmost to settle.

As a prosecutor, he was merciless; as an opponent he could be savagely hostile, but as a man he was charming, and as a friend, he was intensely loyal. In his memorable treatise, *The Art of Cross-Examination*, he demonstrated what his career had fully proven— that he himself was a consummate artist.

MARTIN LITTLETON
(1872-1934)

Martin Littleton was sharply individualistic. With his great heart and emotional response, he was capable of inspiring deep affection and reaction.

He had no difficulty in making friends. Gifted with a fine voice, a mellifluous delivery, and an effective histrionic talent, he was innately an orator. He could make a Websterian address at the slightest suggestion. His early years were spent in defending street railroad damage suits, from which he emerged as an expert trial advocate. He did not profess to be a deep legal pundit, but he was never found lacking in legal authorities when he needed them. His specialty was in the adducing and presenting of facts. He could build those up into a broadside for defense or attack. The stirring force of his oratory and the compelling persuasion of his argument left no one unmoved, not even his adversary. His speeches were as dramatic as a great play, where, without affectation or seeming effort, he rang the changes.

To describe him merely as effective would give scant credit to his performance. He could turn the mind by melting the heart. While by no means an amateur in the technique of a spirited trial, he was likely at any moment to sweep away all doubts and questions by the flood of moving eloquence which he seemed to have ready, for he could pour it out at will. He always had in reserve a body-blow which he might land at any moment and which his opponent must be indeed strong and dexterous to withstand. Hence, he was no mean antagonist in any case where individual rights and wrongs were involved. This gave him remarkable power and rare effectiveness as a counsel for defense. In the Sinclair case he surprised the entire American Bar by the force of his oratory.

Littleton had great human sympathies. For him life was one grand adventure. He did not bother too much about the future, feeling confident that he could always acquit himself satisfactorily in the present. He was an inspiring companion, a hard-hitting fighter, whipping up into a fury then dissolving into compassion at will. Martin Littleton never failed to make a great speech. Whatever the occasion, he dignified and elevated it when he pronounced his oration.

There were no half-tones to his nature. He put his

whole heart into everything he did. When at work, he was indefatigable. Once that work was over, he could play quite as intensely as he had worked. He had the makings of a great political personage, yet after one important civic office and a term in Congress he forsook the political arena. He was not gaited to the regimen of steady effort. He did not enjoy routine.

Without fear of hard situations, undaunted by staggering difficulties, he was ever on the alert for human issues, where emotions were involved, where his heart appeals could sway the judgment as he wished. He was about the last of those rhetorical practitioners who had once graced the Bar. Because of his appealing manner and his remarkable skill in stirring his audience, one never felt that he was striving for an effect. He seemed much too sincere to be suspect.

It was a delightful experience to hear him plead. No matter how dull and commonplace the subject, he could lift it out of its apathy and make it scintillate. He could vivify it into a thrilling situation, for he thought in pictures, and, reflecting them with his fascinating diction, he would build up a grand climax which not even his adversary could withstand. This talent made him more effective in trials than in appeals, more successful with juries than with courts.

As a partner he was difficult. He abhorred a large,

confining office. Office work irked him. But in a courtroom he was in his element. There he was uncontrol-
lable. Interruptions could not hamper him. When he
had an objective in mind, nothing could deter him.
Jurors, when faced with the fire and charm of a By-
ron, the dignity and loftiness of a Cochran, forgot
the client in their admiration for the pleader. He
would place the entire case on his own broad shoul-
ders, carrying the load alone, merging his client's
cause into himself. Every juror would be eager to
measure up to what Littleton expected of him. Careless about his personal affairs, interested rather in the
romances of life than in its trivialities, he was more
poet than barrister, but with a saving sense of humor
which was always effective.

One incident in which he resorted to humor rather
than to the oratory which was expected of him occurred
when he was chosen to be the speaker of the evening
at a Jefferson Day dinner. Each speaker was to be
limited to twenty minutes. Littleton's address was to
come last. He was preceded by a Southern Congress-
man who indulged in rather fatuous remarks for
more than an hour. The dinner guests became restive;
not a few seemed ready to depart. When Littleton
rose to deliver the address of the evening, to the surprise of everyone he announced very quietly that as
the hour was late, he would merely tell a story. It was

as follows: His father had been a farmer in Tennessee, raising stock and grain; one day a traveling salesman endeavored to interest his father in a new patent food for hogs. "Well," said his father, "we have no trouble in feeding our hogs. We give them what is left over and they thrive on it." To this the salesman responded: "But this food is better than any other. The hogs fatten on it in half the time." Thereupon his father replied: "What is time to a hog?" And with this, Littleton sat down.

In his habits he was inclined to be rather quixotic. He loved contacts and he delighted in conversations with those whom he favored with his friendship. Envy and jealousy were foreign to his nature. With a humane heart, his unselfish sympathies were always responsive to the poor, the suffering, and the unfortunate.

He seemed never to compare or to measure himself as against others, and he was always the most generous in the rating of his adversaries. With him rivalry did not mean animosity.

He was brilliant but unpredictable. He had instinctive sympathy with the under-dog and an innate generosity which colored his whole life. Those who heard his addresses could sense the ring of generous kindness in his voice, the light generosity in his face. As Johnson said of Goldsmith: "He touched nothing that he did not adorn."

His favorite theme was that injustice, if countenanced, would destroy the foundations of moral principle. And he had a great knack of instilling moral principle into any argument that he might make. On one memorable occasion when he was arguing an important motion before Justice John Proctor Clarke (later Presiding Judge of the Appellate Division), he gave a thrillingly emotional argument which held his hearers spellbound. At the conclusion of his argument, Judge Clarke announced that he regretted that he would be obliged to decide against Littleton because he had so deeply enjoyed his masterful oration.

Littleton's great vitality, his enormous individuality, and his tempestuous fluency, very seldom failed of their objective. He lost but few cases, and even in those his performance was truly magnificent. With all his great endowments he had a never-ceasing disposition to play and to indulge in divertissement.

He had an innate generosity toward friend and foe; he thought nobody should indulge either in anger or in deep antagonism when the play was over. Seemingly indifferent to the acquisition of wealth, he was fortunately favored with great cases from time to time which enabled him not only to employ his transcendent endowment but to enjoy the good things of life. A great orator, a powerful advocate, Littleton was truly a "Sir Galahad." He will long be remembered for his many remarkable trial victories, especially in cases which, before he undertook them, seemed well-nigh hopeless. Those defeats, which of course he had, were so rare and so few that nobody can now recall them.

Martin Littleton was an accomplished artist who always produced a masterpiece. But it was never a conventional masterpiece, for each was a fresh, original, thrilling and magnificent "tour de force," although always "Littletonesque."

WILLIAM TRAVERS JEROME
(1859-1934)

William Travers Jerome was a fearless individual who never doubted the justice of his objective, a scholar of fine breeding and distinguished background, an able advocate, and an outstanding municipal reformer. He won the hearts of his fellow citizens, and, single-handed, armed only with the consciousness of the right, and the will to win, independently on a lone ticket and without political organization to sponsor him, he upset a Democratic stronghold, though himself a Democrat, and brought order out of chaos.

His first objectives were the gamblers who infested New York City—the giants who had large means and wide influence. He literally chopped them down with his own strong arm. Having only the authority of a police magistrate, he awakened the city to the power of justice and the law. Regardless of party affiliations, he asked and received the co-operation of all thoughtful citizens, and then fully justified the respectful confidence of the community. Once, in office, he called to his staff a remarkable collection of young, ambitious college men, and sent the political hangers-on and the ward politicians out on a long vacation. Surrounded by his earnest, admiring devotees, he produced a new crop of able practitioners, who influenced the entire Bar and resuscitated the administration of justice in the Criminal Courts. During his years of hard battling against disheartening odds, he became invincible to such an extent that even when every voter for him had to write in his name on the ballot for his re-election, he emerged victorious. During the Hughes investigation many great figures were discovered indulging in practice on the verge of the law. He disdained to strike down a prominent man just because his head would be a triumph. He refused to be swayed by public clamor. He declined to twist facts or to indulge in casuistries in order to fashion them into seeming infractions. Those forces he fought remorselessly for years were now arrayed against him, and having, as they thought, found a chink in his armor, they opened a vicious attack and obliged him to defend himself. He came out victorious, but his magic was gone.

In his day Jerome was one of the most individual and picturesque characters in public life. With all the advantages of culture and background, he chose, as

District Attorney, to live modestly in the slums of a downtown district where he would be accessible day and night. There he assembled about him his able assistants, entertaining them with his fund of stories, even personally preparing for them choice food from a chafing dish which he delighted to operate. He would ask them about their problems and give them sage advice. He would discuss with them his personal opinions of the Bench and the Bar. He would hold forth on the art of trying cases, the likes and aversions of jurors, and the new constructions in criminal law.

He had quite some experience as a defense lawyer at the Criminal Bar, as he had been counsel for the notorious Carlyle Harris and in the spectacular Gardner graft case, in both of which he was pitted against the adroit Francis Wellman. As District Attorney, in certain of his important prosecutions, Jerome would himself often take over. None of his able staff was more effective in a trial.

The case of Harry K. Thaw intrigued him. Foreseeing that insanity must be the defense, he became an expert on that subject. He undertook to conduct the prosecution alone. So thoroughly was he convinced that Thaw was a paranoic that he himself suspended the trial at the middle and called for a sanity investigation wherein he as District Attorney attempted to prove Thaw to be a paranoic.

But the Commission, then appointed by the court, declared Thaw sane; whereupon Jerome was obliged to proceed with the trial of a defendant on the assumption that he whom he himself had contended to be insane was sane. After many vicissitudes, and much against Thaw's wishes, Thaw was finally defended by Martin Littleton, and was acquitted on the ground of insanity. He was immediately committed by the trial Judge, Justice Dowling, to Matteawan, the state institution for the criminally insane. Shortly thereafter Thaw started a succession of *habeas corpus* proceedings to prove his sanity. On each of some half-dozen attempts, Jerome would appear in opposition and always defeated the application. One day Thaw escaped, and attempted to get into Canada through New Hampshire, but was remanded to New Hampshire. After a legal fight which went to the Supreme Court of the United States, he was extradited to New York, and tried and acquitted by Mr. Stanchfield for illegal escape. As soon as Thaw walked out of the courtroom he was clapped back into Matteawan under the original order for his commitment.

At the intercession of Senator Philander C. Knox, the Thaw family lawyer, Mr. Stanchfield was induced to undertake a new habeas corpus, wherein he succeeded in getting a jury to advise the court as to Thaw's sanity and thereby delivered him out of the toils of the law. This was entirely new practice but was sustained by the highest court. On this occasion it was not Jerome who opposed him, otherwise the result might well have been different. When I later asked Thaw whether he had any animosity toward Jerome, he replied: "None whatsoever. He only did his duty as he saw it. If it had not been Jerome, it would have been someone else perhaps not so much of a gentleman."

Militant as Jerome was in his prosecution of crime, he was equally alert to prevent an injustice. The most painful experience of his career was that unsuccessful attempt to remove him because of alleged favoritism in failing to prosecute some of the financial leaders.

The outstanding situation in which Jerome showed his fairness had to do with George W. Perkins, a partner of the Morgan banking firm who had been a high executive in a prominent life insurance company. Perkins was a very able, public-spirited citizen who took an active interest in all matters which, as he believed, affected public welfare, and which included some political activities. There was no possible question as to his integrity, but merely a technical doubt as to the proprieties. Public clamor was loud to instigate criminal proceedings against him. While Jerome might have initiated secret Grand Jury action, he chose to thresh out the matter in a magistrate's court, where everything was public and from which an appeal could be taken through all the courts. The result justified Jerome's sense of fairness. The public learned what Perkins had done and the Courts decided that there was no illegality involved.

It was Jerome's lot to prove to his community the immense power which lay in a conscientious District Attorney. But with all his development of that power, he would never consciously abuse it. He was a lofty example of what a District Attorney could and should do, as well as what he should not do. Had he been more ambitious politically and less scrupulous in his activities, he might well have achieved the highest political offices. Above all, Jerome was ruled by his conscience, not by motives of personal benefit or popular acclaim. He was a cultured American who did his duty as he saw it and had no fear of consequences.

Jerome had the gift of clear, terse statement without any obvious attempt at oratory. He would appeal forcibly to reason, and his logic was always most telling.

On one occasion he had a controversy with a clergyman named Kerr who accused him of deliberately permitting the sale of liquor out of legal hours. To this man he wrote the following forthright letter: "Mr. Cur: You are a liar, and you know it. (signed) William Travers Jerome."

He was an able, upright official, who took his job very seriously, spurning the schemes and wiles of the politician. In his day he was the highest type of sincere, conscientious reformer, who revived the self-respect of his community and taught the evil-doers that the law was more powerful than the most potent politicians. As a private practitioner he was unchanged from the man who had been the most formidable of prosecutors. Like so many other outstanding prosecutors, he failed to duplicate his achievements when he became counsel for the defense. It would seem that in the psychology of prosecution there is little if any similarity to that of defense. And Jerome was known as the "Prosecutor par excellence"; as such, the memory of his striking career has never been dimmed by any of his successors.

Jerome preferred to punctuate the defense with simple but destructive questions which were truly devastating. His arguments consisted of an accumulation of testified facts which would leave but little hope for the defense. Judges of the Criminal Court regarded him with great respect and unquestioned confidence, for his motives were always sacrosanct and he would never willingly be a party to an injustice. Scathing as were his tactics where prosecuting, he was never vindictive or cruel. When it came to the matter of sentence, Jerome was always sympathetic with, and sensitive to, any explanation which might modify the severity and rigor of the law, for at heart he was a kind and humane man.

In the history of the American Criminal Courts it is probably a fact that there has never been a more effective and fearless prosecutor, nor one who was more appreciative of human frailty and temptation. William Travers Jerome was a figure of whom New York City may well be proud, for he was the arch type of the conscientious, unswerving District Attorney whom neither fear nor favor could sway from the strict performance of his duty.

Having been a public idol, he loved to see successors, who, without his great ability, seemed to rival him in popular appeal. He was destined to outlive the great public acclaim which he had once enjoyed in so large a measure. But never did he voice regret or discontent, nor did he by word or action intimate that he felt the ingratitude of the public or lamented that his great efforts had failed of due appreciation. When he retired from public life he seemed quite content to rejoin his practitioners at the Bar, there to satisfy himself with the employment of his talents in a private practice without eliciting unusual public attention. In the list of great Public Prosecutors there have been few with the high moral scruples, the keen forensic talents, the deep sense of public responsibility, the sincere spirit of fair play, and the genuine responsive humanity of William Travers Jerome.

EDGAR T. BRACKETT
(1853-1924)

Edgar T. Brackett came from somewhere in the Middle West and settled in Saratoga, New York. He was a rather short, stout man, with a square, well-chiseled, florid face, piercing blue eyes, high complexion, and such hair as he had was red. He looked more like a minister than a lawyer. As a close student of the Bible and Shakespeare, he was ever ready with endless quotations from both with which to point his remarks. He was also a serious student of the classics. When he fought a case, everything went into that fight.

Single-handed, he had driven the gamblers out of Saratoga. Well known for his forensic power over courts and juries, it was a dangerous experience for any lawyer to meet him in combat in his home town. But he had had no experience in New York City. He had two great objectives in his life; one to sit as a Court of Appeals Judge; and, failing that, to practice in New York City. Missing the first by the merest margin, he was the keener to realize the other.

When Mr. Stanchfield died, there were a lot of untried cases that had been paid for. I suggested to Brackett that he come to New York and become a member of our firm. He readily accepted.

Charles T. Morse had just been pardoned out of Atlanta. He was prosecuted again for something else, and indicted and Brackett was appointed a special attorney general to prosecute it. One of Morse's lawyers was a prominent Democrat, a friend of President Wilson, and they began to get uneasy, because they were afraid they'd be involved. One of them came to me and asked me to get them a hearing from Brackett. I said I didn't like to ask my partner to do anything he didn't want to do.

I said to Brackett: "You are a partner of mine, I can speak to you freely, and if you think I should not have told you this, forget it. Don't feel I am trespassing or that I am trying to influence you."

So I told him the story and he said: "Don't fear about telling me anything you have on your mind, and you can talk to me as you can talk to your own father."

Brackett was a man of no shades of opinion. He was either all for you or all against you. No lawyer ever studied his cases more, or was ever better prepared. When he cross-examined a man he tore him to pieces.

Though an uncompromising antagonist, Brackett was as magnanimous in victory as he was contrite in defeat. His principles were high, but in his methods he missed nothing of the skilled artifice of one who knew every device in the trial of a case or in the argument of an appeal. A battle for him was a contest of wits; he went into it like a trained warrior. But the Fates were against him in New York City. He had hardly gotten set for work when his health began to fail. One long siege followed another, and he realized that his ambition was thwarted. With his usual sense of fairness he asked to be released from his firm.

He was the last of those three grand advocates which upstate had given to the City of New York: John G. Milburn from Buffalo, John B. Stanchfield from Elmira, and Edgar Truman Brackett from Saratoga.

As one of the prosecuting counsel in the Sulzer impeachment, his summation will be remembered as the high point of blistering and scintillating denunciation.

As one reads the story of great American advocates, it is striking to find many similarities between Senator Brackett and the famous Rufus Choate. Had the former timed his entrance into New York City some ten years earlier, his record would have vied with any of that city's giants at the Bar.

One story, probably apocryphal, indicates his alert resourcefulness. It is said that he was impanelling a jury in an important case when he came to a name which seemed familiar. It was a common name, but the place of residence caught Brackett's eye. Turning directly to the young man, he asked but one question: "Are you one of the sons of Jim Brown who lives back of the village?"

"Yes, sir," answered the talesman.

"Well," retorted Brackett, "any son of Jim Brown is good enough for me in any case."

It was said that Senator Brackett could squeeze the last drop of benefit out of any situation; that he never missed an opening or an opportunity, never failing to make a spectacular display of great abilities. In an era of outstanding barristers Senator Brackett should fairly be ranked with the greatest.

On one occasion, when a New York bank failed, Brackett proceeded for some stockholder clients to sue the directors. All the directors, save one, made a settlement. That one was George J. Gould who, taking the advice of a prominent New York specialist in banking law, decided to fight the suit on principle. Brackett pushed the case vigorously, obtaining a judgment for the full amount, and sustained it through all the Courts. This was a job which made the leading practitioners of New York City sit up and take notice.

He was in truth a dangerous opponent. His hearers would find it difficult to resist his moving arguments, instinct with a fervor so genuine that it seemed almost blasphemy to harbor a doubt. He would have been a powerful Revivalist, with his knowledge of Holy Writ and his abomination of evil. No one could more luridly paint the blessedness of Heaven or the horrors of Hell.

As a master of jury tactics, with his unfailing dramatic instinct, he had an unerring appreciation of a trial or an appeal. With him, pathos was mingled with persuasion. An admixture of ridicule, irony and sarcasm, fell from his withering tongue in an eloquence of oratory. While a staunch believer in the power of logical argument, he could indulge in denunciation so terrific as to be cataclysmic; yet he could be truly sympathetic and even generous when he thought the occasion warranted it. In his interpretation of facts and their significance, his arguments would seem to be irrefutable. But above all, he hated corruption, especially corruption in public service.

He wielded a power in the Courts where he practiced which could not be denied and which was rarely withstood. No bit of evidence would seem too trivial under the strong light of the exposition which he could give it.

He was quite as able in preparation as he was in presentation. Few knew or appreciated the intensive study and the exhaustive research to which, as a careful student, he devoted himself prior to his every appearance in Court. His assistants might bring him the material, but the task of sorting out the essentials, and of determining their precise use, was performed by him and by him alone.

Brackett was one of the old-style country lawyers. Equally facile in trial and appeal, most effective in any sort of legal controversy, glib of tongue, blistering in argument, at ease and persuasive on any subject whether of law or fact. But the day for his great qualities had passed. It was like the old family doctor and the specialist. When the country practitioner came to the city, he found the tempo quite different. No longer was every passer-by a neighbor. He did not even know the tenants in the office next to his own. The Judges and the juries were all strangers. He realized that he would have to start all over again. And he was quite willing, even eager, to do so. But the toll of the years was against him.

He is not to be judged by his short career in New York City but rather by the brilliant upstate record to which he devoted his lifetime.

JAMES C. McREYNOLDS
(1862-1946)

James C. McReynolds was a little known practitioner at the New York Bar when he was appointed Attorney General of the United States by President Wilson. I first met him when we retained him to prepare the appeal brief in the Patterson National Cash Register case. That contact was renewed when, after Mr. Stanchfield's passing, he sought me out with the suggestion of joining my New York firm.

He had made a noteworthy record of success as government prosecutor in Sherman-Law cases against powerful corporate combinations, all of which had been defended by the ablest legal talent of the land. Woodrow Wilson, the author of the "Seven Sisters" legislation of New Jersey, which was designed to restrict and limit the activities of large aggregations of capital, was attracted by him. McReynolds became a member of Wilson's cabinet. Soon thereafter it was rumored that he was not in complete harmony with the Secretary of the Treasury, William G. McAdoo, then growing in political importance and later to be the President's son-in-law.

One day the Bar was startled to learn that Attorney General McReynolds had been promoted "'upstairs" by appointment to the United States Supreme Court. Instead of following his supposedly progressive ideas, Justice McReynolds became immutably conservative. Gradually but surely he developed into the most conservative member of that august Court. The great corporations which had feared him so much as lawyer and Attorney General came to regard him as their last refuge. He was a staunch believer in the freedom of American enterprise, looking with alarm at increasing governmental interference. Two progressive members of the Court—Justice Holmes and Justice Brandeis— came constantly to grips with him. Later Justice Cardozo also was likewise frequently his opponent on that Bench. McReynolds took their opposition much to heart.

He found the life of a judicial recluse irksome and disheartening. While he was devoted to his work, believing that it was his duty to defend great American enterprise in accordance with his sincere convictions, he longed for the freedom of private life. Hoping that he might find relief at the New York Bar, he asked my opinion and invited me to Washington to discuss the idea. He said he was ready to resign and to engage in private practice with me. As his friend I was conscious of an obligation to be frank, much as I esteemed the suggested association. I told the Judge that I disapproved of the idea solely on the score of his welfare. I pointed out that the rough and tumble of controversy would not be congenial to one who for so many years had enjoyed the authority of that great tribunal; that while he would be best fitted to practice before the United States Supreme Court, his opportunities to do this successfully would be severely limited; that without a McReynolds on that Bench his conservative views might not receive a very sympathetic hearing. The Judge reluctantly abandoned the idea. He realized that this was neither my lack of appreciation of his favor nor a reflection on his high abilities, but a realistic presentation of the prospect he might have to face.

That his advice and advocacy would be sought by important clients was not to be doubted. The disturbing question was this: if as a Justice he was encountering so much opposition in his court, what could he reasonably expect to meet as an advocate? That he could be induced to change his principles and adopt the doctrines of his judicial opponents he did not consider a possibility. He could have returned to the trial arena in which he had earned high repute in his earlier days, but active fighting in trial courts no longer had any lure for him, and he would have had great difficulty in adjusting himself to changed conditions.

We had had an interesting experience with him many years before. It was after Patterson and his associates in the National Cash Register Company had lost their case in the Cincinnati trial before Judge Hollister. Our firm, having been retained for the appeal, decided to secure McReynolds' able assistance on the preparation of the appeal brief, inasmuch as he had recently won a similar case for the government and was thoroughly conversant with every phase of the law involved. When the task was offered to him, he expressed his pleasure in accepting it. Then came the first Wilson election. A few weeks later McReynolds reluctantly declined the retainer for a reason which he gave me in strictest confidence; he was to enter the new President's Cabinet as Attorney General, whose function it would be to uphold the National Cash Register conviction. As he had not started work on the appeal and had not even read a brief or been given a record, he was not in any way disqualified from taking the case against us.

While on the Bench Justice McReynolds was a strong partisan for the views in which he devoutly believed. While he has been classed as a disciple of the Old School, it was as a believer in the New School that he rose to eminence. Once his views were settled, he stood like the Rock of Gibraltar. It was not that his mind was closed, but that after full consideration he had reached a fixed and clear judicial policy as to his duty.

He was a warmhearted and staunch friend who served in time of need. On one occasion when the husband of a childhood friend was on trial in New York City and needed a character witness, Justice McReynolds left his Supreme Court seat in Washington to testify in a lower State court in New York City as to the high character of the accused. He said that he offered his evidence not as a favor, but as a sacred duty.

No other Judge has been more roundly berated because he held out against the latter-day doctrines. But opposition failed to shake Justice McReynolds. It made him more steadfast and less disposed to compromise. Those who disagreed with his tenets as a Judge were obliged to respect the rugged integrity, the unflinching consistency of the man.

As the bitterest opponent of the "New Deal" among the Supreme Court Justices, he aroused President Roosevelt's sharpest antipathy. This was probably one of the main reasons why the President wished to reconstitute the Supreme Court. The retirement system, which at the President's instigation was eventually installed, did bring about Justice McReynolds' retirement.

It has been said that while deep down he admired the learning and the talents of his able opponents on the Bench, he took their opposition so much to heart that his social contacts with them became strained. In this respect, he had the temperament, the courage and the persistence of Andrew Jackson whom he much resembled. He had the same fervor for his beliefs, the same antagonism toward his opponents, and the same forcefulness in his determination. There is a legend of an old ex-slave who guarded Jackson's grave. When asked whether he thought the General had gone to heaven, he replied: "I reckon if the General got his mind sot on it, he got there!" It was resolution such as this which characterized Justice McReynolds. Of such stamina were the founders of the nation.

Judge McReynolds was typical of an age when the United States Supreme Court was called to decide the regularity and authority of unusual national legislation of a novel progressive character; and, at the same time, it had the opportunity to pass judgment upon the regularity and consistency of such legislation as part of the settled national policy. Advocates as well as critics of each school could always find constitutional ground in support of their opinions. An Act of Congress which, to the judicial mind, overstepped the established limitations of the functions of that arm of the government, could always be found contravening the spirit and traditions of the Constitution as developed by more than a century and a quarter of interpretation.

McReynolds had little difficulty in bolstering his vigorous dissents by constitutional and judicial authority. In the latter years his main opponent was Judge Cardozo, who believed that the Court was not justified in reviewing national policy, but should only pass upon the constitutional power of Congress to enact the legislation under review, not whether it was wise or unwise. Therein lay the major contention between the approach of these two schools. The one followed the spirit of traditional principles as laid down over the years; the other rather deferred to the will of the people as expressed by their delegated representatives, if conformable to the prescriptions of the law.

Preceding Cardozo there had been Judges Holmes and Brandeis who had espoused a somewhat similar progressive philosophy; yet occasional instances appeared wherein even they had to interpose a veto against an overreaching by the legislative and executive branches. If the uncompromising differences between these jurists are carefully examined, these will be found to have been their main point of departure.

Each advocate promulgated his philosophy with the fervor of an evangel, believing that the question was vital to the future welfare of the nation. Among the "Nine Old Men," McReynolds was the foremost of the Old School, as Cardozo was of the New.

Justice McReynolds had neither doubts as to the correctness of his attiude nor patience with those who espoused new ideals. Regularity of decisions and fidelity to precedents were, in his mind, fundamental. The basic principles of our government, as he understood them, were, in his judgment, immutable. He considered the Supreme Court to be the bulwark against legislative changes which altered time-honored practices and indisputable principles; that it was the guardian of the people against invasion of their rights; and that all radical or progressive legislation, which ran counter to the policies which had been hallowed by past decisions, should be narrowly construed and cautiously applied.

McReynolds would not have developed the Federal "Police Power" as it stands today, nor would he have permitted the power of the Federal Government to absorb practically all of the State powers which for more than a century had stood intact, until the inauguration of the "New Deal" and the extension of Federal taxation. He considered the established limitations and restrictions, which fenced in the powers of the

Federal Government, to be as honored and as inviolate as the Constitution itself.

Despite his militant attitude and his tendency to take to heart the sharp judicial differences which arose at his Court, Justice McReynolds was a most sociable individual. He was by no means an ascetic, for he was keenly appreciative of the fine things of life, sympathetic to friendships, but unwavering and immutable in his convictions. Congress, at the instigation of the President who was desirous of inaugurating the "New Deal," might retire him but would never be able to change him.

He was in spirit a "Latter-Day" patriarch. He sought neither popularity nor popular acclaim. As a veritable Luther, there he stood, unshaken in his resolute fidelity to the creed which he believed, with a fervent faith, which, in his mind, admitted no doubt or question.

IRVING LEHMAN
(1876-1945)

Irving Lehman had an excellent background and a fine education. Having had but little court experience, he was nominated on the Democratic ticket and elected as a Supreme Court Justice in New York City, to the surprise of the public, to whom he was practically unknown.

It is doubtful whether Irving Lehman ever personally tried a case before he ascended the Bench. Moreover, he suffered from partial deafness, and the Bar, quick to capitalize on a disability, would humorously say that in his Court an objection would be "over-heard" instead of "overruled." He took his time to decide and was punctiliously thorough in his research and meticulously careful in his decisions. Before long he had impressed both the Bench and the Bar by his learning, his fairness, and his industry. Serious lawyers with important cases would jockey them so as to ap-

pear before him. Among the scores of trial judges in
the State of New York, he eventually acquired a reputation second to none.

His deafness and his deliberateness were more than
compensated for by the quality of his work. He considered the law to be a science. He kept in step with
all the multitudinous decisions appearing both here
and abroad. He worked over them as minutely as a
scientist would work in a laboratory.

Judge Lehman was not disposed to ask for personal
recognition. He was, however, blessed with an able,
charming, ambitious helpmate, who, convinced of his
outstanding abilities, was determined that they be
fairly appreciated. While he was quietly attending
to his work as a trial Justice, a vacancy occurred in the
Appellate Division to which, in due course, the Governor would make an appointment. His wife, anxious
for her husband to be considered, came to me, having
known me socially, and asked my assistance. I told
her that I had no political connections, and that, with
every desire in the world to help, I did not know how
to start.

She said: "Don't you know Mr. Guthrie well? He
could help a lot." I replied that I did know him well,
and that I would be glad to speak to him about it.

Whereupon I enlisted the support of William D.
Guthrie, then a recognized Bar leader. He promptly

agreed that Judge Lehman, on his record and his ability, was entitled to sympathetic consideration. But he later reported to me that the incumbent members of that Court had already asked for the appointment of Judge Francis Martin. Guthrie still offered to press the Lehman candidacy, but Judge Lehman modestly declined to have him do so, stating that he did not wish any action on his behalf to be taken counter to the will of the Judges of that Court.

This decision, however, turned out to be very fortunate for the Judge. Not long thereafter a vacancy occurred in the highest court, the Court of Appeals, owing to the retirement of Judge Hogan. Judge Lehman's wife resolved to press for his selection. Again she sought me out, and between us we got in touch with the Republican and Democratic organization heads. After much difficulty and many counter suggestions Judge Lehman emerged as the nominee of both parties.

Governor Miller, being no longer in office, was then the recognized head of the Republican Party. I went to him first. He agreed that Judge Lehman was, in his opinion, the best possible man for the post.

Lehman's father-in-law, the venerable Nathan Straus, had been a life-long Democrat and was still influential with the Democratic organization. He had supported his Democratic friend, Hugh J. Grant, for Mayor of

New York City. He had also induced Democratic President Cleveland to appoint a brother, Oscar S. Straus, as Ambassador to Turkey.

But despite Governor Miller's persistent endeavors, he was informed that the Democratic nominee should be a Roman Catholic, as the retiring Judge Hogan had been the only Roman Catholic on the Bench. In vain did the Democratic organization, through former Judges Edward E. McCall and Morgan J. O'Brien, strive to move ex-Governor Miller, even to the point of suggesting that he might name any Roman Catholic he chose, who would receive the nomination of both parties. But former Governor Miller, true to his promise, refused to endorse anyone but Judge Lehman. His insistence ultimately prevailed.

Judge Lehman proceeded to make an outstanding record. First as its member, and later as its Chief Judge, he upheld the highest traditions of his office. No advocate ever left Judge Lehman's court feeling that he had failed to obtain from him a fair and unprejudiced hearing. His decisions were models of industry and erudition. With the courage, if not the boldness, of Cardozo, of whom he was a devoted follower, Lehman turned neither to the Right nor to the Left.

While Cardozo was concerned in the shaping of the Law, Lehman was intent upon its correct interpretation and application, regardless of the trend. One of the proudest moments in his life was when, as Chief Justice of the highest court of the State, he administered the oath of office as Governor to his distinguished brother, Herbert H. Lehman. In the long line of its honored incumbents, no court has had a record purer, more circumspect, or more honorable than that of Irving Lehman. He may justly be deemed a worthy successor to Cardozo.

His opinions had not the trenchant, limpid charm of Cardozo's. Whose but Justice Oliver Wendell Holmes' did have? They had not the dynamic force of Cullen's. They had not the suggestive progressiveness of Pound's. But they were matured with solid learning. He was a fine example of what hard work and sincere ideals, with great ability, can accomplish, even when compared with the attainments of genius.

With all his studious habits and his scientific procedure, he was always human. No capital case on appeal to his Court failed to receive his conscientious consideration. He would himself read every word of the record, and only if he were convinced of the guilt beyond doubt would he vote for affirmance. Each request for a hearing in his Court he would examine patiently and carefully, so that every possibility of error would be thoroughly explored. Whenever there was room for doubt, he would grant the right of appeal.

From the moment he took his seat on the Bench he gave himself completely to his work. Aside from his charities, which he considered a duty to the community, he took no sides and espoused no causes. While he had been a devoted protege of Al Smith, he was also a sincere admirer of Franklin D. Roosevelt.

As Presiding Justice of the Court of Appeals he became a very wise and careful administrator. He might differ vigorously from some of his colleagues, but he always respected their independence and encouraged their freedom of expression. In his desire to promote the continuity of judicial rulings, he was still sensitive to the development of the law, though innately opposed to the disturbance of its authority. Under his careful interpretation, the laws of the State became a settled jurisprudence, not subject to whims, fancies, or innovations. He gave the law a stability, reducing the element of chance and increasing the degree of certainty.

Bacon's famous precepts for Judges were scrupulously observed by him:

"Judges ought to be more learned than witty; more reverend than plausible; and more advised than confident."

"Patience and gravity of hearing are an essential part of justice."

All knew that he was endowed with a fine intellect, that he was an unremitting worker, and that his motives would never be suspect. But the erudition which he acquired, the impartiality which he displayed, and the executive ability with which he discharged the duties of his office, astonished his most enthusiastic admirers. He was a disciple of *Stare Decisis,* a follower of Justice Story rather than of Chief Justice Marshall.

As a careful student of the American and English law, he had a broad grasp of the decided cases and a sincere appreciation of the legal philosophy which entered into them. Fearless of criticism, his conscience was his guide. For the acknowledged leaders of the Bar he had unfeigned admiration; but he would give the same courtesy to an unknown lawyer as he would to a leader.

Irving Lehman has left an inspiring memory of what can be accomplished by devotion, by tireless industry, and by the conscientious performance of duty. In every thought and in every action he was, in truth, a fine Judge—an honor to the Bench which he so ably graced. His unselfish career and his unswerving devotion, as shown in his decisions, to the duties of his office, are indeed a monument to his memory, more lasting than stone or bronze.

THE AUTHOR

AND SOME OF HIS FRIENDS

Figure 1: Louis S. Levy 1877-1952

Figure 2: First Board of Editors, Columbia Law Review, 1901

Seated—C. Boardman Tyler, Treasurer; Joseph E. Corrigan, Editor-in-Chief; John M. Woolsey, Sec'y; Louis S. Levy, Bus. Mgr.

Standing—George G. Schreiber; Harold Walker, Decisions Editor; Herman F. Robinson; Forsythe Wickes; Beverly R. Robinson; Burton W. Wilson.

Figure 3: The author with Winston Churchill.

Figure 4: The author with Bernard Baruch.

John B. Stanchfield 1854-1921

Figure 6: The author with Samuel Untermyer.

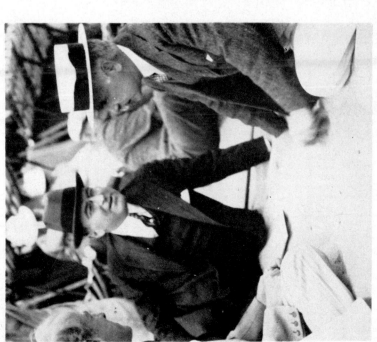

Figure 5: The author with Otto Kahn.

Figure 7: August Heckscher, friend of the author.

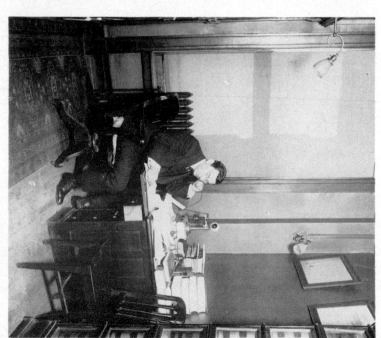

Figure 8: The author — an early study.

Figure 10: Louis Wiley (left) and Lord David Duveen.

Figure 9: The author with Grover Whalen.

Figure 11: The author with Alfred E. Smith.

VICTOR J. DOWLING
(1866-1934)

Victor J. Dowling began his career as a political leader, and as such he wielded a powerful influence in the New York State Senate where he was the designated representative of the New York City organization. After he resumed private practice he served faithfully in my firm as our learned counsel as long as he practiced. Subtlety and subterfuge were foreign to his nature. If anything, his habits of mind were almost too impartial and too judicial to permit of the partnership required of a practicing lawyer. As an advocate he was still a Judge, for it was impossible for him to espouse any cause with which he was not in complete sympathy.

When elected a Judge, his closest associates were amazed by his industry and studious attention to his judicial work and by his complete detachment from all political connections. Nobody suspected the ability

which he then displayed. He had been regarded as
a routine political appointee. Rapidly he gained prestige as an able jurist. Before long he was elevated to
the Appeal Bench where he finally became the Presiding Justice.

He brought to the work a keen and educated mind.
His opinions were learned, decisive, simple, and framed
in clear diction. Courteous and patient as he was on
the Bench, no human appeal left him untouched. Yet
he was careful and fearless, prompt to make a conscientious decision, with no stubborn pride of opinion.
He was a pillar of his Church, and a recipient of the
highest honors bestowable on a layman, as well as a
learned ecclesiastical scholar.

Practically his single Court appearance was on the
personal request of his friend Cardinal Hayes for a
boy who had been an inmate of Irvington House, an
institution for cardiac sufferers. He fell into bad company and was used by a gang who set out to rob a
jeweler and ended up by murdering him. While this
boy was not a participant in the actual crime, the gang
had used his car and had later parked their artillery
with him. When apprehended, the active perpetrators
saved their lives by pleading guilty, leaving this for-
lorn lad to face the murder charge alone. By being
subjected to personal coercion, he was induced, in
order to help his wife, about to give birth to a child,

to sign a statement which implicated him with knowledge of the robbery plan. He was convicted of murder in the first degree and condemned to death. It
was the final plea in the highest court which Dowling
was induced by Cardinal Hayes to make. There he
distinguished himself, winning a reversal for which
his only compensation was the satisfaction of a task
well done.

In his last days Judge Dowling was appointed a
receiver of the I.R.T. Street Railway System of New
York, where he could quietly and effectively employ
his talents.

Judge Dowling's studies were not confined to the
law which he was chosen to administer. He was an
intense student of French literature, of history, and
of the canonical law. He was an ardent patron of
the theater, a man of esthetic culture. About his personal affairs and tastes he was almost a recluse.

That those who knew him personally appreciated
his superior talents was shown by his selection as a
Trustee of the great Equitable Life Assurance Society.

Though he was at ease on the Bench, he shunned
participation in the fighting arena. He could charge
a jury superbly but he could not argue with one. As
a Judge, he could bring up a witness sharply but he
could not cross-examine him. He was an arbiter, not
a gladiator. After leaving the Bench he was quite

ready to give wise and practical counsel, to analyze
complicated facts and decisions, to furnish helpful
suggestions, but always for others to execute. It was
not that he had any trouble in thinking clearly and
quickly on his feet, or in expressing himself readily.
But there seemed to be for him some hurdle in the
battle itself which as a protagonist he wished to avoid.

Judge Dowling was an example of clever politician
turned able jurist. It was undeniable that it was his
prominence in State and City politics which led to
his election to the Bench. Determined to do all his
research himself, he gave personal attention to the
business before him, writing his own opinions, de-
clining the assistance of the law secretary which the
State provided for him.

Year by year his influence increased and with it his
reputation. When at the end he became the Presiding
Justice of his Court, there remained no doubt as to his
eminent fitness for that post. When he retired, it was
generally considered a distinct loss.

Dowling had been obliged to work hard for all he
attained. He was not born amid affluence or indulgence.
Sheer determination and fidelity to ideals impelled
him to develop his superb mental equipment. He never
forgot the hard conditions of his earlier years. His
keen intellect could grasp the most tenuous distinctions,
without disregarding the main objective. With him,

theory was always subordinate to facts, ignoring neither expediency nor principle. His wide learning did not obscure his common sense. While he was erudite, he was always practical. The vast business in his Court he administered with solemnity as well as with dispatch.

There was never difficulty in getting to him with any matter which merited his attention. Once he saw his duty, he was neither hesitant nor afraid. Self-interest or personal advantage never entered into his deliberations. With consideration for all, and an open-mindedness which welcomes any deserving plea, he became the model for an appeal Judge. His subsequent career in private practice was too short to afford an adequate opportunity for his talents.

He had little experience in transacting business affairs. In his personal matters he was as simple as a child. His lack of familiarity with industrial and commercial problems led him to look with amazement upon those who were skilled in such matters.

With a delicately balanced mind and a devotion to duty, he had the predisposition of the monks of old. In his work he preserved the sanctity of a monastery. A gourmet in his habits, he never became gross or unrefined. Cardinal Hayes was his adored intimate friend. None of his secular honors equaled, in his judgment, those which he enjoyed in the Church.

As a Judge on Appeal, he was always ready to grant Certificates of Reasonable Doubt, believing that it was only humane that a convicted person should remain at liberty so long as his Appeal was pending.

No Judge was more careful in following the trend of decisions and none was more humble in bowing to the adjudications of higher courts. He never complained of reversals. There were no animadversions in his work.

Victor J. Dowling was a splendid example of what an American citizen with but little background to start with could accomplish by the development and application of his native talents. He proved that firm determination, conscientious hard work, and strict devotion to duty bring the rewards of outstanding achievements.

His career was indeed a source of justifiable pride to the Church, to the Bench, to the Bar, to the City, and to his political party.

GEORGE L. INGRAHAM
(1847-1931)
MORGAN J. O'BRIEN
(1852-1937)

Outstanding jurists of their time were George L. Ingraham and Morgan J. O'Brien, both originally trial Justices, then appointed to the Appellate Court, each in turn became its Presiding Justice. These men, both during their tenure of office and after leaving the Bench, were intimate friends and social companions of Mr. John B. Stanchfield, and so I had unusual opportunities for meeting them, for learning about them, and for listening to them. After their retirement from the Bench they both appeared frequently as counsel with our firm, and in such work their talents and their propensities were readily discernible. It was then that I came to know them intimately and to appreciate their sterling personalities.

In appearance and nature these two men were al-

most exact opposites. Ingraham was slender and ascetic; O'Brien robust and full-blooded. Ingraham was
a somewhat difficult Judge before whom to plead.
Overwhelmed by an avalanche of business, he was
fretful of delay, intolerant with those who seemed to
be wasting time, resentful toward those who assumed
to tell him what he had theretofore decided, but quick
to grasp any new point and to weigh any serious argument. He preferred to direct the argument rather than
to await its orderly development. He took his function
very seriously; he could be short and caustic when
annoyed. Yet he was a careful, scholarly, conscientious
Judge, though not so beloved as O'Brien, Ingraham
would incline toward a narrow view, if supported by
established authority; for he disliked to disturb the
settled precedents. He was theoretical and legalistic,
aiming at a conclusion consistent with prior decisions.

O'Brien was more practical and less studious. He
was warm-hearted, having the objective of substantial
justice, without too much regard for precedent. He was
moved by his heart, Ingraham by his mind. Ingraham
was less easily approachable but more set and incisive.

In their intellectual attitude toward a legal problem
their divergence was equally noticeable. Ingraham was
the technical schoolman, the industrious researcher;
O'Brien the man of the world, always seeking the
human element, eager to square his conclusions with

his sympathetic instincts rather than with the books. Yet after many years together on the same Bench, and despite their fundamental differences, each entertained a genuine respect for the other, and each had an effective influence on the other. There was no other Judge for whose learning O'Brien had greater esteem; when it came to settled decisions, he would unquestioningly accept Ingraham's report. Similarly, in considering the effect of a decision in the special case at issue, Ingraham would often yield to O'Brien's humane views. Together they made an excellent combination. There were not bitter dissentions, no antagonisms, but always good feeling and genuine co-operation.

Ingraham had a social following among the elite of the Bar. Among the rank and file O'Brien was the more popular. Men like Root, Hughes, Guthrie, and Nicoll were drawn to Ingraham; Littleton, Wellman, Untermyer, and Steuer felt closer to O'Brien. Stanchfield, however, was truly fond of them both. O'Brien was one of his bosom friends, but he had no greater admirer on or off the Bench than Ingraham.

It should in fairness be noted that Ingraham's tenure had the more constructive influence. As Presiding Justice his administration was the strongest and the strictest since the days of Van Brunt. That office, so important for the orderly and expeditious handling of its voluminous litigation, was the busiest and most

complicated judicial post in the State. For many controversies, this was the court of final resort. Except for
capital cases, all the litigation of the heart of the greatest city in the land had to pass through it, and much of
it got no further. It needed as its President an able
executive, an industrious administrator, one learned
in precedents, who could be judicial, consistent, and inflexible. These qualities were more conspicuous in Ingraham. He established a high record for order and
regularity. Though somewhat of a martinet, he
achieved many undeniable benefits and developed a
fine working system. While O'Brien had respect for
order and system, he was more inclined to relax a
rule which he thought inadequate for a special case.

Both were Democrats who laid aside all political
considerations once seated on the Bench. Ingraham
was the son of a distinguished Judge and the father
of another, all Democrats. His was a judicial family.
O'Brien had first received a political appointment
(early in life through the auspices of his influential
brother-in-law, John D. Crimmins) as Corporation
Counsel of the City of New York, and from there as a
Democratic nominee he went upon the Bench. O'Brien
rarely appeared in Court. Occasionally his name would
appear on an appeal brief, but he would not willingly
participate in a trial or argument. Ingraham would
not try jury cases, but was eager to make a legal argu-

ment in any court. Yet he could not realize the difference between the role of the Judge and that of the advocate. He would still be the jurist expounding the law in his rather pontifical manner, not always too deferential to the Court whose function it was to decide. O'Brien was disposed to disregard decisions which offended his instincts, was likely to give them too little attention, then to run afoul of them. He was more resourceful in practical suggestions, while Ingraham was the more erudite. If a careful, exact exposition of the law be desired, none could furnish it better than Ingraham; if an ingenious plan or a strategic policy were needed, O'Brien could supply it.

Ingraham was scholastic and unyielding; O'Brien was practical and pliable. Ingraham was governed by decisions; O'Brien by the sense of fairness. Ingraham was impatient, inclined to be intolerant with an unscholarly presentation; O'Brien was indulgent, sympathetic, eager to help out an advocate who struggled with the intricacies of his case. Ingraham was strict while O'Brien was tolerant. Ingraham was diligent, always busy with his work; O'Brien was easy-going, seemingly without worry and never oppressed by the duties of his office. Ingraham looked upon his responsibilties as a paramount moral duty, while O'Brien took them in his stride, undisturbed, and with a feeling that it was all in the day's work. Ingraham was a man of few indulgences, seemingly with few personal pleasures, not one whom you could slap on the back or carouse with; O'Brien was by nature a boon companion who heartily enjoyed comaraderie and all the indulgent pleasures of life. Ingraham was inclined to be a hermit, while O'Brien craved the company of his many friends, loving the association with them.

With Ingraham, advocates must always be prepared to the hilt, else they would receive a rough reception. With O'Brien, they need only touch the high spots. Ingraham was an independent thinker who could be an intolerant dissenter; whereas, O'Brien always seemed inclined to follow rather than to lead, unless worried by a feeling in justice or impressed by the over-reaching of a litigant. Together they were a wonderful combination.

In their long periods of service both made splendid records for the volume and the quality of their work. As able public servants, they both performed their tasks honorably, and gave lavishly of their high ability. Both earned and enjoyed the respect and confidence of their community in a superlative degree.

Judge O'Brien had a great knack of inducing his friends to do certain work which he found irksome. They seemed to take pleasure in doing things for him. When it came to fees he was so modest as often to defeat himself. In a certain large case involving millions, where he had been retained by my firm to act as counsel for one interest, he was asked to fix his fee. He named the sum of $2,500—far less than he was entitled to. I, who had retained him, said that his fee should be at least $10,000 in a case of that magnitude. O'Brien responded that he could not ask that much. I explained that there had been millions involved and that while he had not been required to devote much time, it had been necessary for him to master many intricate facts and to take a firm stand, re-inforced by his position and his authority, the effect of which had been largely instrumental in securing for his client a very favorable result; and that there was no possibility that the client would object to a very substantial fee. I told Judge O'Brien, in support of my argument, that a smaller fee would merely result in the client's lack of appreciation of his service. He finally agreed that $10,000 would not be exorbitant in view of the result obtained. I said that if he would call with me on the client, he need say only one word: "Ten," and he would get a check for that amount without argument.

At the appointed time and place we met the client who greeted us pleasantly. I mentioned first that the fee had been discussed with Judge O'Brien. I asked him to say how many thousands he wished. O'Brien, with considerable hesitation, finally managed to say

$7,500. Thereupon the client expressed his gratitude, saying that the fee was extremely moderate, and promptly gave him a check for that amount. The additonal $2,500 would have been paid quite as cheerfully had the Judge been able to say that one word: "Ten." As the Judge left with me, he privately apologized to me saying that he did not have the nerve to ask for more than $7,500, which amount he considered a generous payment.

When, because of age they retired into private practice, each joined a large, active, and important firm. Each was frequently sought as counsel in important cases. Rarely has it been found that an able Judge on retirement becomes an effective advocate. There would seem to be a fundamental difference in their approach to the task as well as in their technique in its doing. True, judicial prestige may serve to attract those who seek learned legal opinions. But the facility for arranging facts, for building up situations, and for emphasizing those controlling features which so often turn the scale, would seem to be almost unknown to the ex-Judge. With only a few outstanding exceptions a retired Judge finds it difficult if not impossible to adapt himself to the exigencies of private practice. Such, in a considerable degree, was the experience of both Ingraham and O'Brien. While they brought stability and authority to their respective firms, they did not match their judicial records by their achievements in private practice. They earned more money but much less prestige.

For these men the job of Judgeship was a sacred function, as solemn as a religious commandment, and just as strictly to be observed. The bitter political fights of a great city often came before them in litigation; but no trace of politics every swayed their judgment. Each took his service as a sacrament; each left a splendid record without a single question as to his unwavering and unsullied integrity. With our multitude of judicial incumbents, such records are too soon forgotten; but theirs will bear the severest scrutiny and should serve as a proud example for their successors. Their difference in temperament seemed to place each in greater relief. Their qualities were supplementary. Each in his own way was a fine Judge. Between these two able jurists, justice was neither blind nor careless.

ELIHU ROOT
(1845-1937)

Among the outstanding lawyers of yesterday were
some whose rare talents placed them in a special category. They not only knew the law and propounded it
learnedly; they were legal engineers who pioneered
new paths, who understood the fundamentals of great
institutions, of Commonwealths, and of nationwide
trends; who could both blaze new trails for us and
guide us along the old ones. They have sometimes
been called "constitutional lawyer," but this phrase
inadequately describes them. The lawyer who argues
the meaning and force of a constitutional provision is,
strictly speaking, a constitutional lawyer. But the abilities of some transcended these narrow limits.

Such a man was Elihu Root. One could not converse
with him without sensing his tremendous mentality,
his extreme tolerence, and that essential democracy
which, though it typified the man, never made him

a popular idol. He was a tall, spare individual, with one eye slightly off-center, a high-pitched voice, and a rather austere and frigid manner. His features were as regular and as sharply cut as those of a Roman senator. He was fundamentally a statesman. His knowledge of the aims and purposes of the Constitution resembled that of Chief Justice John Marshall; his knowledge of precedent and legal theory was like that of Justice Joseph Story. Despite his rather aloof manner, he had an understanding of human nature of the quality of Abraham Lincoln. Withal, he had the humor of a Joseph H. Choate but without that mordant wit.

Although he was not a politician, he had once been Republican political leader of New York City, and was adept in the political game. His personality did not have a popular appeal but those in high office were aware of his unusual ability, and they had the wisdom to select him for his great qualities. Among the outstanding services he rendered were, as Secretary of War under President McKinley, continuing as such under President Theodore Roosevelt; and then as Secretary of State under President Theodore Roosevelt; finally as United States Senator from New York.

As Theodore Roosevelt's constant advisor on many matters, Root was capable of steering him safely and surely through every serious situation. If all the facts were known, it would be found that much of the success of Roosevelt's administration was due to the presence of the ablest, shrewdest, the most far-sighted, and the most delicately balanced legal philospher and statesman in the nation. On one important matter President Roosevelt did not seek his advice—in his break with President Taft. Root sternly disapproved of this action. It shocked his sense of party loyalty. It was his firm opposition which stopped the Rooseveltites in the Convention of 1912 that nominated President Taft for re-election. This led to Roosevelt's nomination on the "Bull Moose" ticket, and to the defeat of both candidates, thereby electing Woodrow Wilson.

As Roosevelt's Secretary of State, he visited the South American republics and laid the firm foundation for the "Good Neighbor" policy. His international notes were a model of clearness, firmness, and deference to American traditions. It was fortunate for the nation that, after leaving the Cabinet, he entered the United States Senate. There he served the nation with his profound wisdom and sage advice on every grave question which that body had to consider. He was, beyond question, the ablest and most dominant figure in that august body. Among his loyal followers, upon whose respect and unwavering support he could always count, were many able members of the Senate, such lawmakers as Sutherland, Lodge, and Borah.

When President Wilson went to Paris to settle the peace treaty after World War I, it was suggested that he take Root with him, not only as an influential Republican, but as the best-informed American on national and international affairs. Had this suggestion been accepted, it is probable that President Wilson would have been spared the Senate repudiation of his plans for a League of Nations, as Root openly favored such a League. Senator Lodge, who became its chief opponent, was ever a devoted Root follower, who yielded to none in his deference to Root's wisdom. Later, when an international court was to be established, Root was chosen to lay it out.

While Root was accustomed to large fees, he was not always careful in collecting them. When he was retained with John G. Johnson in the John R. McLean will contest in Washington, D. C., our firm was selected to conduct the litigation. The contestant was Edward B. McLean, son of the testator who had been cut out of his father's will. The contest promised to be long and bitter unless these eminent counsels found a means of adjustment agreeable to both sides. A satisfactory compromise was ultimately effected. But when these counsels sought to collect the fee which young McLean had previously agreed upon in writing, he declined to carry out the agreement, offering them nothing. The alternatives were either to sue or to dismiss the matter as a bad debt. Despite the enormous amount of work done and the satisfactory result, the counsel decided to drop the matter. Root said that while he did not wish to prevent his colleagues from taking action, for himself, he "would be satisfied with a doughnut," as the whole amount involved would not compensate him for the annoyance of a personal lawsuit.

In the course of the McLean negotiations there was a meeting at Senator Root's New York apartment attended by Frank Hogan and another prominent Washington lawyer in support of the will, and I was with Senator Root, attacking it. Hogan became quite vehement and rather abusive in characterizing the attack; so much so that his associate, in deference to the Senator, interrupted him. Thereupon the Senator quietly remarked: "Please do not stop him. The young man seems to know what he is talking about. So let us hear what he has to say." In due time the Senator courteously but effectively answered Hogan and deftly brought about a complete adjustment of the will. It was his tolerant courtesy quite as much as his argument which effected the result.

Outstanding among Root's achievements was a new constitution for the State of New York. At the Constitutional Convention, at which Mr. Stanchfield was a member, and over which Root presided, the latter was considered by all, regardless of party, as the ablest, the most constructive, and the soundest in that galaxy of solons. It was here that he complimented Alfred E. Smith, then an Assemblyman, as being the best informed individual, truly an expert, on State functions.

Root challenged the Eighteenth Amendment as being inconsistent with the principles of our Constitution and pernicious in conception; for, while he was always temperate in his habits, he opposed the principles of Prohibition.

His connection with the Tweed case is now recorded history, although the public has long neglected to inform itself on the details, all of which are highly creditable to Root. When William M. Tweed, the notorious political boss of New York City, found himself charged with crime, he selected for his defense the leading members of trial bar, with whom Root and Willard Bartlett (later Chief Justice of the New York Court of Appeals) were associated as juniors. It was an outstanding case for which, as a matter of professional distinction, any young lawyer would have been glad to be chosen. The case appeared for trial before Judge Noah David, who had been newly elected to the Bench on an anti-Tweed platform.

All the counsel for the defense realized the handi-

cap of a trial before a judge as to whose antagonism
there could be no doubt. As a last resort and in the
interest of an impartial hearing, the defense counsel
made a formal protest at the opening of the trial by
a Round Robin, setting forth with due respect and
solemnity their objection. The trial Judge calmly read
the protest but made no comment except to say that
he would attend to the matter later. After a bitterly
contested trial, Tweed was convicted. It was only then
that the Court adverted to the Round Robin. The
Judge ordered all the signatories to show cause before him why they should not be punished for contempt. After hearing their responses, he found them
guilty; he fined them all except Root and Bartlett,
whom he excused on the ground that, as they were
very young men, they had undoubtedly been influenced by their more experienced associates to join in
the protest. But Root made no such defense. He stood
professionally upon his rights; he argued that he had
done only his duty to his client. In future years it became the habit of his detractors to refer to him sneer-
ingly as the "Tweed lawyer." But the practice of urging
the prejudice of the Court is today fully recognized
and specifically authorized in our Federal system.

As legal counsel he disdained to waste his artillery
on trivial points however vulnerable they might seem.
He had the faculty of reducing the most complicated

situations to their ultimate essentials. When he cast
the light of his powerful intellect on any subject, it
was illuminated even in its murkiest corners. Given
his premises, his argument was unanswerable.

On one occasion when we brought him the will of
the first Marshall Field, disposing of a great estate,
but holding it in abeyance for two generations, and
therefore subject to justifiable attack, he opened the
discussions by exclaiming: "When will our rich men
learn to leave their estates to their heirs rather than
to the Bar?" When he was asked his opinion as to
the chances of success for the heir seeking to acceler-
ate his large but long-deferred inheritance, he answered: "This young man is likely to receive much
more money than is good for him."

The Field Case had a curious history. The grandson of the first Marshall Field had brought it to us in
the hope that we might find a flaw which none of the
many other lawyers could find, so as to secure for him
some sorely needed funds. Mr. Stanchfield first gave
the Marshall Field will to several of his distinguished
friends on the Bench, asking them to study it, and to
give an opinion, for by no chance could the matter
ever come before them in a judicial capacity. Each of
them reported that there was no possible ground for
attack and no discoverable loophole. He told me that
I *must* find some ground for its attack. After weeks of

intensive study, I hit upon a single ambiguous clause of the long, cumbersome will.

The will provided that if one of the grandsons died, the entire residuary estate should go to the other grandson. Then a separate clause followed directing that it be held subject to the same trusts as were thereinbefore provided as to "each" of the grandsons. That word "each" implied more than one, and yet there was only one grandson left, for the younger grandson had died. So the language of the testator could not possibly be carried out unless the word "each" were to be construed as meaning only one — the single survivor of the two grandsons. This, in my opinion, gave rise to a serious ambiguity which inhered in the very heart of the main bequest.

When I reported this to Mr. Stanchfield, his opinion was that the point was almost too slender to defeat such an elaborate document; but he was not hopeless of utilizing it as a leverage for prying loose a substantial portion of the estate for the benefit of the client. He declared that we must make up, through the heaviness of our artillery, for the lightness of the ammunition. Accordingly, he suggested that we retain the great Elihu Root, universally conceded to be the leader of the American Bar, and, as the case must come before a Chicago court, John S. Miller, the outstanding barrister of Chicago, together with his associate, the learned former Judge Edward E. Brown, also of Chicago; and, in addition to this formidable battery, Professor Charles A. Collin, former Dean of the Cornell Law School, an indefatigable law researcher.

It was our good fortune, through Senator Root, to have the able assistance of his partner, Greenville Clark, and also the late Robert P. Paterson who was later to become a Federal Judge and Secretary of War. This strategy, approved by Senator Root, eventually resulted in tremendous advantage to the heir in that memorable contest, thereby proving the accuracy of Senator Root's remarkable forecast and the wisdom of Mr. Stanchfield's far-sighted generalship. That it was an outstanding victory of that era can hardly be questioned. It resulted in a beneficial change in the Illinois law, whereby the long-deferred enjoyment of estates such as was contemplated by the first Marshall Field is no longer permitted.

An instance of the prestige of Senator Root was the occasion when an attempt was made to oust the Guggenheim control from the American Smelting and Refining Company, in which contest I was engaged as their counsel. During the United States participation in World War I, the market price of metals, especially of copper, rose steadily; and the Smelting Company accumulated a huge quantity at these high prices. Following the cessation of hostilities, there was a sudden, rapid, sharp decline in the market. The company then faced a large loss in its very considerable inventory of metals.

A committee of objecting stockholders was organized to seize control, under the leadership of Henry Evans, an influential sponsor of important fire insurance companies, and Clarence Kelcey, the highly respected head of the Title Guarantee and Trust Company, prompted and advised by Carl Eilers, an experienced engineer who had been for many years Vice-President of the Smelting Company. The campaign of attack which ensued involved the responsibility and efficacy of the company management which had never been previously questioned. Being anxious to relieve the stockholders of a harmful and expensive fight, the management suggested that all questions be submitted to Senator Root as arbitrator. But the Evans group declined to accept this proposal. Thereupon the management itself alone submitted the whole matter, with all the facts and charges, to Senator Root, publicly agreeing to abide by his decision.

Senator Root went to work at once. He personally examined all the charges and made his own investigation of the facts. Then he rendered his written opinion, completely absolving and exonerating the management of any blame of mismanagement. His opinion was so clear, cogent, and exhaustive that when

published it effectively disposed of the entire controversy quite as conclusively as though he had acted as
an arbitrator. This significant incident indicates not
only the supreme ability of the Senator, but likewise
the respect and confidence in which he was universally held. Probably no decision, short of the highest
Court in the land, could have been so effective.

But for all his colossal stature at the Bar, he never
bore down on his opponents, nor did he attempt to
overwhelm them by his prestige or his learning. He
would meet the humblest adversary on a level, patiently
and tolerantly presenting his views, trusting to his
logic rather than to his authoritative importance.

As proof of his open mind and his progressive interest, it is noteworthy that, while the "New Deal"
was contrary to the tenets of his lifetime, he expressed
the keenest interest in its theories, and predicted that
many healthy and helpful reforms would emerge from
its seemingly radical tendencies. He knew that the
nation would neither refuse it nor be "stymied" by
its process.

Beyond doubt the greatest lawyer of his day, and
possibly the equal of any lawyer of any day, he not
only rendered great patriotic service to his country
but left his noble example for generations to come.
It is a strange turn of events that Root, whose assistance as advisor at the Paris treaty negotiations was de-

clined by President Wilson, should later be selected
as the recipient of the Woodrow Wilson Foundation
Award for "meritorious service to democracy, to public welfare, to liberal thought, and to peace through
justice." In the history of that Foundation there has
probably been no other recipient who more richly
earned its award.

Root's mentality was not only analytical; it was
creative. He was a master both of theory and practice.
He viewed the nation not only in its constituent parts,
but in the international setting. He regarded liberty
and justice as the life-line of the world. While he
knew the frailty of human nature, he envisioned its
enormous potentialities under competent leadership.

Cardinal Newman's description of a "balanced
mind" in his essay on "The Idea of a University"
aptly characterizes Senator Root:

> "He is never mean or little in his disputes,
> never takes unfair advantage, never mistakes
> personalities or sharp sayings for arguments,
> or insinuates evil which he dare not say out.
> If he engages in controversy of any kind, his
> disciplined intellect preserves him from blun-
> dering discourtesy. He may be right or wrong
> in his opinion, but he is forcible, and as brief
> as he is decisive. He knows the weakness of

human reason as well as its strength, its province and its limits."

Elihu Root was an outstanding statesman with the gift of pre-vision, conversant with the intricate laws of nations; a great rationalist with an ideal mixture of realism and idealism. His outstanding qualities were his clearness of vision and his forthright belief in America and its people.

He had many sides to his great character which evinced a remarkable resemblance to the Founding Fathers of the United States. His serenity was like that of Washington; his simplicity similar to Franklin's; his democratic principles like those of Jefferson, and his facility in government machinery like that of Madison and Hamilton. No man more admired the strength of character, the knowledge of history, and the unflinching courage of Woodrow Wilson than did his opponent, Elihu Root.

While not a great orator in the sense of a Webster or a Clay, he was a much greater statesman than either of them. When Franklin D. Roosevelt announced the doctrines of the "Forgotten Man," it did not shock Root. He stated openly that there might be a great deal of sense in that idea and he awaited with keen interest the outcome of that philosophy, believing that it would bring about many needed reforms and great benefit in the nation.

Far from being a sentimental or effusive politician, he neither sought, nor was he swayed by, what may have been a popular trend. The transcendent attributes of power that his activities disclosed were the result of his wide study, his sensitive understanding, and his profound intellect. Looking back upon the current of his years and unceasing fertility of his achievements, it is amazing that such intent perception and keen evaluation could remain alive for so long a time.

His later years were devoted to the private practice of the law, with such opulent clients as Thomas Fortune Ryan, Andrew Carnegie, and the Theodore Roosevelt family. Eagerly he was sought by all who had great causes and difficult problems. He was the architect of the Carnegie Foundation and for many years its most influential spirit. It was at his suggestion that funds were given to Dr. Banting and Dr. McLeod to produce "insulin," that life-saving remedy for diabetes.

His opinions might be questioned, but his integrity and patriotism, never. His illustrious career demonstrates what the sheer mental power of one great man and its wise application can achieve, without trace or suggestion of demagoguery or of personal exploitation. He asked nothing of the public but he gave to it, generously and unstintedly, of his unrivaled talents. If one might venture to rate all the leaders of his time, it must be conceded that Elihu Root is entitled to a place in the very front rank, indeed to the very first place, though this may be placing more emphasis on integrity, singleness of purpose and patriotism than seems to be the habit today.

JOHN G. JOHNSON
(1841-1917)

John G. Johnson was the appeal counsel "par excellence" of his era. As a constitutional lawyer, in the strict sense, he was the leader of the American Bar. No other man appeared more often in the most momentous cases before the highest tribunals. Serving in a period when "Big Business" had so many restrictions and legal hurdles to overcome, he was their habitual advocate, and none was listened to with more respectful attention. The Sherman Anti-Trust Law, in its manifold applications, was his specialty. He became an extra-judicial authority as to what large corporations could or could not do legally. As counsel for the Wideners, the Elkins', and the Dolands of Philadelphia, with their widespread interests, he became their "Excalibur."

In the myraids of intricate corporation questions which were involved in his era, no advocate rendered greater service in the development and construction of the law; and none enjoyed greater prestige. He had one strange quality. No lawyer charged less for his small services or for those which required little attention, and none received larger fees for great cases. Often when retained by other lawyers, among whom our firm enjoyed that privilege, his meager charges became a thorn in the side, because the charges of others loomed so large when compared with his.

His remarkable influence in the Supreme Court decisions is evident from the fact that, even when unsuccessful in persuading the whole Court, he generally succeeded in winning over a minority of its members. His wealth of knowledge of the individual precedents, of the spirit and application of the law, was always of tremendous help to the Bench.

While Johnson was truly a learned appeal counsel, he did not shine as a trial lawyer. He was more of an analyst. His talent did not lie in the give-and-take before trial courts and juries. It was on an appeal, where a careful, scientific analysis of facts and law was essential, that he was the arch advocate. In this work he was truly a jurisconsultant of the greatest eminence, in which respect he resembled Elihu Root. He did not frame constitutions, nor did he lay out international courts, but no other man could better demonstrate the meaning and intent of a constitutional or

statutory construction, or better elucidate the spirit
of the law.

Johnson had some unusual idiosyncrasies. He disliked to dictate his memoranda, briefs, or even his
letters. He preferred to write them out in longhand,
in writing so illegible that often he himself was unable to read it. His experienced secretary could usually
decipher it more readily than he could. He also disliked to transact business by telephone. Except for
short messages and appointments, he held his conferences in personal meetings.

He was an ardent devotee and an industrious student of art. Emulating his great Philadelphia clients,
Widener and Elkins, he assembled a remarkable collection of Dutch, Italian, and Flemish masterpieces.
Without paying the enormous sums which his clients
expended, he made a collection of more than a thou-
sand pictures, many by the finest outstanding masters,
and all selected by him alone. It has been said by one
competent to judge that he was the best informed of
all the great collectors of art. In his later days, though
his eyesight failed him, he never lost his ardor or his
interest in art. Seated in the front room of his unassuming home on South Broad Street, in Philadelphia, which was literally filled with paintings from
floor to ceiling, even in the vestibule and halls, he
would point to each of his favorites and learnedly dis-

course on its beauty, its origin, and its meaning. At his death he willed the entire collection to the City of Philadelphia. It is carefully preserved in a museum, where it will ever serve as a memorial.

Johnson was a bachelor, rather short and portly in stature, with a full gray mustache. He could be courteous or curt, as his mood happened to be, but he was always kindly and understanding. Having stated his opinion to the Court with his supporting reasons, he would seldom argue it further. Always decisive and accurate, he approached the law as a science, and for it he had a scientist's respect. With those who treated it as a game, or an opportunity for trick or artifice, he had no tolerance. Because of the coolness of his temperament and the steely sharpness of his mind, he had an almost uncanny prescience when it came to forecasting judicial reactions. The confidence of Bench and Bar and the unswerving loyalty of great clients gave him an eminence rarely attained in our history. It could not be disputed that no other man of his time could more ably and effectively present his cause. Failing health and poor vision did not check his ardor nor slow down his activities. He was in truth a law architect who knew all the bastions of the law; who was familiar with the strains and stresses; who had a clear understanding of its basic purpose, and could expound the meaning and intent of those who

added extensions as well as of those who formulated
the original plans—all he could shape into a homo-
geneous structure. He conceived the law as a living,
logical instrument. He differed from Elihu Root in
that he was the interpreter who could vivify law, while
Root was the genius who could create it.

There was no great constitutional question in the
United States in his lifetime that he wasn't in on. He
would make his argument, and if the judge didn't
agree he would say: "That's my argument; you don't
have to agree, but that's my argument." When the
Steel Trust was founded, it was said that there were
two men consulted—one was Grover Cleveland, who
advised Mr. Morgan it was illegal; and the other
was Johnson, who advised him it was legal.

Johnson was a rare personality, interested in everything which made for enlightenment and culture, al-
beit he was a person of frugal tastes and ascetic habits.
His pleasures and diversions were entirely intellectual.

His minute knowledge of the basic legal principles
could not be questioned. When he undertook to discuss their origin and development, his presentation
was comprehensive, exact, and rational. Moreover, he
could marshal the most intricate and complicated facts
so that they seemed as clear as crystal. The cases in
which he shone were such as to tax the skill and ingenuity of the proverbial "Philadelphia lawyer." And

that is just what he was, in the utmost degree. In the forge wherein the meaning and purpose of great legislation were hammered out, he was arch-smithy in that difficult and delicate process.

The highest courts were as eager for his approval as he was for theirs. His record furnishes an ideal example for those who aspire to master the science of the law of the land. It is likewise a guide for the piloting of great enterprises through the involved intricacies of the sinuous complexities of the law, since he had a major role in the interpretation and application of the fundamentals of latter-day American jurisprudence. As his reputation with the Bar was nation-wide, so were the beneficent results of his high service. He disdained the arts and wiles of popular appeal. Though well-known only to that limited class especially interested in his field, by them he was universally esteemed and respected as second to none—a veritable giant.

If the reports of decisions of the highest courts in his day be carefully examined, it will be found that under his guidance many of the most far-reaching, momentous, and important decisions were formulated. Therefore, he may be justly credited as the inspiration which induced our highest courts to reach many of their adjudications.

But his influence can hardly be appreciated by reference to decisions alone. For many years, practically

every progenitor of a large corporation or a nation-
wide operation went to Johnson for his sage advice
and authoritative counsel. No matter how wise or
careful a company's counsel, when it came to the
point of indulging in a large, important operation
which involved the possibility of Government interference, resort to Johnson was the ultimate safeguard,
the "Rock of Gibraltar."

Johnson is largely responsible for many of the
most important corporate enterprises of the United
States. While he was not always successful in obtaining the sanction of the high courts, his percentage of
victories in an over-all consideration of the multitude
of his opinions will amply vindicate his authority as
the wisest, safest, and soundest of counsellors on the
many intricate questions that were propounded to him.
He had an abiding principle which he followed religiously in all his work. He would never present an
argument in which he did not profoundly believe.
While the highest court might not agree with him,
he would be forever mindful of that disagreement,
so that never again would he risk the possibility of
defeat; still in his heart of hearts he would be personally satisfied that he had been right and the court
had been wrong.

The complicated law which affected the huge corporations whose cause he espoused grew apace under his

influence; and no other man, not even the highest court itself, had more influence in the growth than he had.

It should be noted that Johnson, while the ablest interpreter of constitutions, was himself not a framer of them. Once formed, none could better pronounce their meaning and effect; but it is doubtful whether he ever formulated an amendment to the laws. He did not see the United States as a nation among nations as did Root. He was not an international lawmaker as was Root. He had not the talent of statesmanship as had Root. But when it came to an argument on a constitutional question, or on some broad principle of law which affected the fortunes and welfare of the nation, no man surpassed him in expounding the meaning and the purpose of constitutional provisions. He had a mind instinct with appreciation for them. He had an intimacy with all constitutional rulings which bore upon his cases. And, most of all, he had the rare gift of being able to illuminate the driest, most recondite constitutional provision in simple but forceful language which left no doubt as to its purpose, construction, and application.

He could take a voluminous record, extending over hundreds of pages, and compress its content into a short, simple, concise statement which did no violence to the evidence, nor was it negligent of, or oblivious to, any vital fact which that record contained.

Neither court nor counsel could ever accuse Johnson of a misstatement or of a garbled version. Scrupulously careful to present the facts as clearly and as succinctly as he did the legal issues, he was a safe and sure guide to the courts, and an adversary with whom there could be no fair dispute as to the meaning or application of a given provision of the law. Merely with the weapons of forceful argument and unassailable distinctions, he illuminated every issue which he presented. No wonder that the higher the court, the higher the respect it had for Johnson; or that every court considered it a rare privilege to receive and to weigh his marvelously compact and instructive elucidation. He was always true to his ideals—ideals as high as those of any lawyer who ever practiced at any Bar.

As Daniel Webster said of Samuel Dexter, in his famous eulogy on January 26, 1830:

"A question of Constitution Law, too, was of all subjects, that one which was the best suited to his talents and learning. Aloof from technicality, and unfettered by artificial rules, such a question gave opportunity for that deep and clear analysis, that mighty grasp of principle, which so much distinguished his higher efforts. His very statement was argument; his inference seemed demonstration."

WILLIAM D. GUTHRIE
(1859-1935)

The rapid expansion of industry in the first decade of the twentieth century brought to the front a great advocate, William D. Guthrie. He was so essentially a student and an exponent of basic legal principles that he, too, is entitled to be classed as a jurisconsult. Beginning as a shorthand secretary, he ultimately became the leading corporation attorney in New York City. Like John G. Johnson, he was more strictly an appeal lawyer than a trial lawyer. He was highly dignified, studiously prim and correct in manner. The Roman Catholic Church which he espoused later in life was very close to his heart. He was always foremost in its protection whenever he thought its well-being or its integrity was menaced. In research and in the interpretation of judicial precedents, no other man of his time was more industrious, learned, or effective.

He was a stickler for form. Resourceful as to all

the pitfalls and the by-ways of corporation law, there seemed to be no complication in any branch of the law which baffled him. While not a criminal lawyer, he could write a brief on a criminal appeal which would be second to none. He had a grasp of legal principles and of judicial interpretation such as is given to few. Whatever the cause, Guthrie could be counted upon to deliver a scholarly argument. His briefs were a model of simplicity and cogency. Over and over again he would polish the language, giving minute attention to every phrase, word, and comma; so much so, that often the last version lost some of the sparkling spontaneity of the first.

Guthrie was scrupulously punctilious about the amenities. No letter failed to get a prompt reply. Personalities he eschewed, and nothing so disturbed him as to suffer them from his adversaries. In all the New York prolific traction litigations and the investigations which for two decades harassed such enterprises, he was the outstanding advocate who skillfully protected their interests.

Like all great advocates he could cut to the core of a question. While temperamentally legalistic, his mental integrity was unimpeachable. His logic was never strained. Listening to his argument, one felt that he was a sure, unfailing guide, steering through the mazes of a labyrinth. While he lacked the scope of

Elihu Root and the power of John G. Johnson, he always gave the impression of a fine scholar. His was the illuminating argument which upset the first Federal Income Tax (1896), when, upon a reargument, he turned the decision by persuading one member of the Supreme Court, Judge Shiras, to come over to the opposition, thereby making the dissenters the majority and the majority the dissenters.

He had great respect and reverence for his profession, quick to rush in to right an injustice wherever he thought there was one. His influence on the Bar was always edifying and inspirational. While not an orator in the sense of a Littleton or a Brackett, yet by clear logic and irrefutable learning alone his pleas were always impelling.

In his later years, he would have liked a high judicial position; but when the opportunity came, as it did, in the offer of an appointment to the highest court of the State of New York, he was too near the retiring age of seventy to accept it. Always engaged in the most substantial corporate controversies of his period, no man was more busily employed, more attentively regarded, or more distinctly helpful in his final adjudication.

Guthrie was a gentleman of refinement and culture. He lived the life of a scholar. His interests were broad, generous, and intellectual. But he had a persistent habit of which few were aware. With his excellent facility in shorthand, he made notes of every important interview, which often served him in good stead.

With his classic face, his handsome features, and his quiet manner, he looked like a typical dominie. No coarse expression, no vulgar phrase, ever passed his lips. He did not believe in prohibition, although he was wholly abstinent in his habits. Cigar or cigarette smoke seemed to suffocate him, yet he would never intimate to his consultants his aversion to it.

He was always sympathetic with the French. He spoke the language fluently and took an active part in all French affairs in America. He was awarded the French Legion of Honor.

He never considered himself too important to discuss freely and frankly any legal questions with the humblest practitioner; neither was he hesitant or unwilling to express his views however unwelcome they might be.

One of his outstanding traits was his patience. His painstaking search for authorities seemed to be limitless. In conference he was never "short" or intolerant. He might not always agree with his associates but he was never lacking in his respect for another's opinion; neither did he ignore or disregard an adverse view. Rather would he summon his learning and his logic as a submission for consideration, instead of attempting to overrule another's opinion. Hence, his arguments generally prevailed, not because of heat or emphasis, but by reason of their inherent merit.

Guthrie was not fully appreciated in his time, nor has he been since. From humble beginnings he emerged a polished, highly educated gentleman. None reflected more sincere refinement. Perhaps inclined a bit toward pedantry from the nature of his studious activities, he had, nevertheless, an unselfish admiration for the talents of others, with an open mind, free of prejudice or bias.

He lacked the illuminating sense of humor such as Root had; nor did he have the latter's breadth of conception. But for sheer learning and the skill of clear, simple statement, he was the equal of any. In the shaping of the intricate corporate law of the land, as construed by the Courts, he was a potent factor. He was in truth a law exponent.

Once his seeming aloofness was penetrated, his company was both a delight and an inspiration. In the rush and turmoil of the present tempo by which the law and all other activities are perceptibly affected, there is too little opportunity to emulate his lofty example, and there seems no longer to be that driving incentive which impelled him. He lived as a gentleman, practiced as a gentleman, and never stepped out of that role. He could forgive any attack on his views but not his principles. Such grievances as he harbored were only aspersions on his intellectual integrity. He was indeed a very fine person as well as a very able one.

Intellectually honest and tolerant, it would be difficult to find any practitioner of his time who upheld more conscientiously the highest standards of his profession than he did. Much of his time he generously gave to movements calculated to improve the standards and the practice of his profession. His door was always open to fellow members of the Bar who thought they were the victims of unfairness or injustice.

Guthrie never enjoyed the popularity and the credit which his unselfish endeavors merited. The Bar, generally, was estranged by his seeming aloofness. There was probably no other man of his day who esteemed the affection and regard of his co-practitioners more than he. No man was more worthy or deserving of them. And yet it is only fair to say than only too few fully appreciated him and his great human qualities.

He often said that next to the Church, he knew of no profession so sacred as that of the law. But he realized that the law was a living thing not to be circumscribed or nailed down by time-worn doctrines or outmoded theories; that it must progress with the genius of the people; that it should change with changing conditions; that it should be sensitive and

responsive to human development; and that, while it
is based on reason and the greatest good for the
greatest number, no man can foretell what future
conditions may arise. He believed that the law should
be settled so far as basic principles were involved.
The mere fact that he could present a scholarly argument as to the meaning and purpose on an existing
law did not, in his mind, in the slightest degree militate
against a proper adjustment of the existing law to the
needs and demands of changing conditions.

But he did not believe that the courts, in our system
of government, had either the right or the power to
change the law; for that, in his opinion, was solely
the function of the legislative. However, he found
many instances wherein the old and revered decisions,
standing as the law for decades, were based on incor-
rect reasoning or the failure of counsel to foretell
new situations which had since arisen. While he was
an uncompromising advocate for the application of
the law as it had been settled by time-honored decisions, he was nonetheless alive to the necessity for its
adaption to the mutations of new conditions and
changing times. He was an intense advocate of the
sanctity of justice, believing devoutly that our system
of laws, inherited from the English jurisprudence, is
the fairest, the most impartial, and the most just system ever achieved by human intelligence.

At one time Guthrie headed what was probably the largest law firm in New York City, one of whose members became a partner of the Morgan banking firm. A difference of opinion in the Plant will contest, which he won for his firm, led to its dissolution and his withdrawal. Guthrie, with a few associates, established his own law firm. He preferred a small personal practice to a law factory. Later he withdrew to a small office uptown where, with one assistant and a secretary, he confined his attention to those matters which especially interested him. He wished to lighten his load but still to keep himself moderately busy. It was thus that he spent the last years of his life, contented and happy.

JULIUS ROSENWALD
(1862-1932)

Of all the philanthropists of his time, Julius Rosenwald, the head of the Sears-Roebuck Company, occupied a unique position shared by few. Starting as a
modest traveling salesman for a clothing manufacturer, he ultimately became the chief owner of this
nation-wide "mail-order" concern, with wealth reck-
oned in scores of millions. Yet with all his resources
he never changed his habits. He would not send a
telegram if a post card would do. He preferred to
travel in a section rather than in a drawing room, objecting not to the cost but to the waste.

Engaged in a highly competitive enterprise, he
would never resort to sharp tactics. He had an abiding
respect for the rights of others. Through his wonderful "mail-order catalogue" he established a new nation-
wide institution. No family was so remote as to be
beyond its reach. The opportunities accorded to city

residents were brought by it to the humblest village, town, and farm home. There was no exaggeration or misrepresentation. Every article was found to be exactly as described. The Sears-Roebuck catalogue became almost as much used as the family Bible. And every patron, even the most humble, was assured of prompt, efficient, and courteous service. While the original idea was not Mr. Rosenwald's, its enormous development and its wide application were his. It was to these that his concern owed its huge success. Yet he was always disposed to attribute that success to his associates. The idea has since been developed and emulated by others, so that his institution is no longer unique. But for character, dignity, and responsibility it has never been equalled. There are many such as Rosenwald the merchant, but few such as Rosenwald the philanthropist.

To him philanthropy was not a kindness, and neither was it a matter for public commendation or exploitation. It was, in his opinion, a privilege given to the doner. He said he gave, not because of his pleasure or his sympathy, but because of a solemn obligation. He truly looked upon giving as a sacred duty to be performed, not the doing of a voluntary favor. I recall a certain meeting to which he asked me to accompany him, where he was told of a projected nationwide drive for funds to aid his co-religionists in Russia.

After the conditions and objectives had been explained, he came forward with a huge amount, not conditionally but as an incentive for raising as much more as possible. He said that he did not wish his contribution to slow down the effort, even requesting that it be given no publicity and that neither his name nor the amount be mentioned. When on the way home I expressed my profound admiration for such generosity, he at once replied: "My dear boy, you have got me wrong. Those people are not indebted to me. It is I who am indebted to them for showing me my duty and for affording me the opportunity to do my duty. No man is entitled to praise for merely doing only what he ought to do."

With his hat in his hand, he would go about Chicago, New York, and elsewhere, soliciting charity by a personal appeal to the conscience, not the liberality, of his prospects. Never boasting, never asking gratitude, he was rather embarrassed when his good work received praise, for he felt he was receiving it under false pretenses.

Here was a truly sincere philanthropist. While visiting the Tuskegee Institute he conceived a deep sympathy for the Negro. He believed that these people who had been brought to America, not by choice, but by compulsion, had the right to ask America to feed them, to give them a decent living, and to provide

them with the opportunities open to their white brothers. In his modest way and without the slightest ostentation, he was moved to assist them by himself giving
freely to them some part of what he considered the
nation owed them. This was not a mere gesture. It
was an honest attempt on his part to remedy a rank
injustice. While he could not hope that his financial
help alone would entirely solve the problem, he felt
it might enlist the help of others, thereby providing
the Negroes with something substantial toward the
betterment of their condition. Thereafter he would
frequently talk with praise about the work being done
at Tuskegee, but he would never mention what he himself had done; indeed he was quite angry when anyone even indirectly referred to his own contribution.

To the Chicago University he donated millions.
Having exhausted his cash for the moment, he made
his gift by delivering a large block of his precious
shares with his personal guaranty of their value. Ru-
mor has it that when those shares were almost at their
nadir, he was "called" upon his guaranty, much to
his sorrow, because he had felt certain that the shares
would before long regain and even exceed the highest value to which they had theretofore attained. But
Rosenwald was a man of his word. He never made a
promise which he failed to keep. While his compliance
with his guaranty involved a serious personal sacrifice

for him, he nevertheless took up the shares, paying the full amount which had been promised.

Free of bias, without prejudice of race or creed, this merchant prince felt himself under a high obligation to share with his fellow men his good and great fortune.

There have been richer philanthropists and those who have given away much more, but the country has never known one who gave more happily and more sincerely, or who was more truly actuated by the purest motives. In his heart, Julius Rosenwald believed that it was more blessed to give than to receive; that he had received only that he might give; that his success carried a stewardship to be honestly performed.

Rosenwald believed wholeheartedly in America, always preaching its blessings and its opportunities. Here was a great man who had built a great company which became a golden boon to his co-venturers; but his greatest gift to his fellow citizens was the loftiness of his example. The epitaph which would have pleased him above all others is: "He did his duty as he saw it, faithfully, honestly, and nobly."

Not to superior ability did he attribute his great industrial achievement, but to a kindly destiny which had appointed him to devote it to worthy ends, in the confidence that he would do so. This trust was a mission in which he would not consciously be derelict. It was for him an obligation which in good conscience he could not shirk.

That he was not concerned with building a monument for himself is plainly evidenced by that mandate in his large testamentary trust stating that within the span of twenty-five years every cent of principal as well as of income must be disbursed. Those terms his representatives have religiously carried out. Regardless of the extent and nature of his philanthropies, Julius Rosenwald's example will stand as a paragon and beacon for all philanthropists.

His many charities have passed. His wonderful institution has grown and will continue to reach heights beyond those which he envisioned. But his imperishable memorial is his unselfishness and the wonderful example left us of that noble spirit which prompted him.

In Rosenwald's philosophy, the highest duty of any individual was: to improve the condition of his fellow men; to aid the underprivileged; to contribute to the general education; to improve the public welfare, rather than to pile up a mound of gold for personal enjoyment. He avoided individual extravagances, for he believed that the wealthy should do much more than enjoy themselves. Accordingly, he was sympathetic and responsive to every just human appeal.

He had no personal conceit, no feeling of superiority, no pride of possessions or position. His great success as a merchant did not change his mode of life. At his zenith he lived as simply and as humbly as he had in the beginning. Moreover, in his theory of giving to others he was not content merely to make his own contribution; he considered it his duty to carry his philosophy to other people who could emulate him. The only pride he ever evinced was in his great establishment; that pride lay more in the service which that business rendered than in the profit which it earned. While those profits have been ever increasing with the years, Rosenwald could not be justly called a profiteer; since he believed in the profit motive as an incentive to success, that the laborer was worthy of his hire, and that in order to continue its great work his firm must necessarily earn profit and ever wider patronage. Rather than boast of his commercial success, he preferred to talk of those early days when he was merely a run-of-the-mill traveling salesman.

The pity of it is that while his great company still enjoys its nationwide patronage, all too few appreciate and revere the noble spirit who directed it to its wonderful achievements, who inspired it by a feeling for humanity—a spirit which has but too rarely characterized the builders of great enterprises.

Wealth had for him no great lure; only the uses to which it was devoted justified its possession. His selfless, quiet benevolence was not, to his mind, the giving of charity, but only the doing of a duty. It was, essentially, the impulse of a noble heart. Its modest integrity was the loftiest example of pure benevolence.

The memory of this noble man should not pass with the distribution of his fortune nor with the cessation of his largesse. Rather it should endure as a deathless inspiration for all who in the succeeding generations may be impelled to express a love for their fellow men. Of Julius Rosenwald it may be said that the sanctity of his religion and the purity of his life were truly exemplified by his whole-hearted performance of the divine injunctions of the immortal Sermon on the Mount.

AUGUST HECKSCHER
(1848-1941)

Among the public-spirited philanthropists whom I should honor is August Heckscher. A foreign-born emigrant from Dusseldorf, Germany, this little man had nerves of steel and a generous heart.

For years he engaged in successful mining operations, mainly zinc and iron, as an executive rather than as an operator. Then he became fired with an ambition to buy and improve New York City real estate. Almost before the public knew of his existence, he had a veritable real estate empire in New York City. At one time he owned both sides of the street near Grand Central Station. No operation was too huge for him; skyscrapers and blocks of apartments were built, bought, and sold by him in abundance. His fortune soared into millions. Yet he remained always the modest retiring man of his earlier days, with no extravagances and no personal indulgences. He never wore a tailor-made suit in his life.

One day he astounded the city by a lavish gift of a beautiful Fifth Avenue building, encompassing an entire block, for the aid and benefit of poor children under the auspices of the Children's Aid Society. Huge in size, equipped with a theater and every latest convenience, it was given by him, free and clear, together with a substantial sum of money for its upkeep and operation. He also gave large endowments to Cornell University and to Rutgers. When, under the Al Smith regime, the Jones Beach project was envisaged, Heckscher voluntarily came forward with a very substantial donation toward its cost, because, as he said, it would bring such a boon to the children of the city.

Then came World War I. There were some who openly questioned Heckscher's loyalty because he was German-born. While he always retained his affection for his birthplace, he was uncompromisingly opposed to the German attitude and lost no opportunity to express that opposition. He promptly sued his traducers for their infamous slanders, and by winning his case, he effectively disposed of them.

August Heckscher had forseen and participated in a great real estate expansion and improvements of New York City after World War I. To secure the immense resources required for such operations he became a very large mortgage borrower. The lending institutions liked him, extending him large loans, amply secured by his properties as he and they believed, and supported by the adequate income which they then yielded. One day the tide turned, and values began to shrink, tenants being no longer able to pay their rents, and the great Heckscher found himself in an inextricable "squeeze."

It was after he had passed fourscore years that this misfortune overtook him. But his courage did not falter. He made every sacrifice, in a desperate attempt to save what he could. He had never realized that reactions could occur in real estate as they did in every other species of commerce. He had measured real estate values by the income returns. Real property, and especially improved real property, he looked upon as an impregnable fortress, able to withstand any storm or torrent. But he was then oversold on New York real estate, whose values, even when most highly improved, could not weather the storm. With Teutonic stubbornness, he refused to recognize the condition which became all too apparent. He disdained to admit any possible errors in his judgment. Those great dreams of his, in which he envisioned the boundless future of America, could not, in his opinion, be wrong. When his ship was in danger, he jettisoned only such holdings as he was forced to relinquish, staking his all on the remainder, hazarding everything he had for the ultimate salvage in which he religiously believed. In the midst of these troubles he was still cheerful, hopeful, generously charitable, and continuing his philanthropies as he reduced himself to little more than the bare necessities of life.

His great properties gradually fell away one by one, and he was finally obliged to part with the monumental Heckscher Building on Fifth Avenue, the idol of his heart, to which alone he gave his name. His last years were sad, because he could no longer do the benevolent things he had been accustomed to doing. With his smaller means, he found that his wings had been clipped. Yet he bore up like the Spartan he was. Life still had great zest for this little man, who would not give up hope, who had, as a youngster, been warned that his life expectancy was short because of a heart condition, but who, by his careful, rational regime, lived well into his nineties.

Heckscher was the undisclosed benefactor for many public and nation-wide movements, all humanitarian, charitable, and non-sectarian in their scope. He was particularly interested in all organizations connected with child welfare, for he believed that such organizations made for better citizens. Likewise he was interested in helping indigent mothers, for he considered that by helping them he was helping their children. He was interested in science and scientific education for which he gave liberally though unobtrusively to scientific institutions. Also, he had many personal charities in which he quietly indulged, helping unfortunate individuals whom he deemed worthy. But while a clever, sharp businessman, keen to ferret out ways to make profits and to exploit them, he would never take an unfair advantage. He was never hard, bitter, or unfeeling. At heart he was a very simple, merry soul, almost boyish in his pleasures, despite his great age. He would dance, sing, and drink beer with the youngsters.

His faith in New York City real estate never waned, even in his darkest hours. But it was his optimism which led him, much as did William Durant's, into over-extension. Canny and careful as he was, his judgment was thwarted by his optimism. Like a winning gambler, he was ready to stake his all on that judgment, confident that he knew how it would eventuate. So many times had he been right that it was generally believed that Heckscher never could be wrong.

His monumental buildings literally dotted the principal streets of the city. He even ventured to erect a huge, costly hotel in Palm Beach, Florida, for the benefit of his son whom he was anxious to encourage. His daughter had married Lord Esher of England and had been given a magnificent marriage settlement, so he felt assured that her fortune was safe. But his son had not been so successful; he had a family of whom their grandfather was very fond and for whom he wished to provide the promise of substantial security. And to the extent which his means permitted, Heckscher never failed those grandchildren.

He had enjoyed a full, happy life and he frequently said that life owed him nothing. In his later dark days he was never heard to complain or to repine. He used to say that he had landed here with very little, had enjoyed wonderful times, and if he left with very little, he would still be much ahead on balance. As to his philanthropies, he never regretted what he had given away; quite the contrary, he said that his one great regret, the unforgivable mistake of his life, was that he had not given away more when he had it to give. It was his belief in the city and its citizens which brought him the rich dividends that he was happy to share with them. He was one of those rare characters who, whatever he might achieve for himself, was always keenly conscious of a duty to others—an essential attribute of a real philanthropist.

Had he been able to hold out a little longer, his optimism would have achieved its most sanguine expectations. But neither his long purse nor his long life was long enough. His fortune, since greatly restored by the holdings he retained, has gone to others of whose existence he could never have been aware.

Toward the end of his life he came to me, asking if it would be seemly for him, at his advanced age, to marry an elderly lady whom he had known for a long time and who had been an intimate friend of his deceased wife. He said she was alone in the world and had been devoting considerable time to him; that she was most congenial, and very considerate of his welfare; that purely out of kind friendship she had given him the pleasure of her company and had kept alive his interest in living when most of his old associates had passed on. I could see that he was deeply moved and that he believed the suggested marriage would bring him much happiness, if only in the companionship alone. I thoroughly approved of the step. His marriage proved most happy, serving to brighten those anguishing dark days when his fortune gradually slipped away and when there was little hope of his regaining it. The lady survived him for only a short time, but she had been his solace and his comforter when he had been in dire need.

While Heckscher's great estate empire has been broken up and widely distributed, his chief benefactions have remained intact. There can be no doubt that if her were given the choice as to which should stand as his monument, he would choose those which still bear, and will continue to bear, evidence of the philanthropy of the man rather than of his clever and bold commercial operations. The latter had been engineered and consummated in order to make the former possible. It may properly be said that Heckscher's life did not result in a failure but enabled him to produce ever-lasting monuments to the charity of his great heart.

Few native Americans had more respect and truer loyalty for the country which welcomed him as a poor immigrant. That welcome he sincerely requited by his unselfish generosity and by that very confidence in his adopted country which proved to be his undoing. Fortunately, his favorite structure stills bears his name; but it should indeed be graven in undying memory and not in perishable stone and steel. The city and the institutions which enjoyed his unselfish generosity should not be remiss in rendering their unending appreciation.

JOHN A. HARRISS
(1862-1940)

Quite unheralded, as a strange personality, Dr. John
A. Harriss sprang suddenly into notice in New York
City. He was called "Doctor," although nobody seemed
to know what sort of physician he was, or whether he
had ever practiced. He emerged out of World War I
with unmistakable signs of wealth. No one knew his
history, where he came from, or how he made his
money. He had a fleet of expensive automobiles, several large yachts, a grandiose country estate in Darien,
Connecticut, and a solid block of houses on Riverside
Drive which had been converted almost entirely into
one dwelling, with a maze of rooms rather garishly
decorated but expensively furnished, in which resided
a curious assortment of elderly men and women,
friends who had seen better days, and who, in this
quiet retirement, enjoyed his hospitality, rent free,
for as long as they chose to avail themselves of it.

When appointed a Deputy Police Commissioner without pay, no other one man did more for the welfare of the New York Police Force. He was a large contributor to the Police Fund, missing no opportunity to give and secure donations for its benefit. He devoted himself constantly to the study of New York City traffic, and he initiated many improvements in its handling and regulation. He was the creator of the present traffic light system. The first traffic towers, made of solid bronze, costing $25,000 apiece, were developed and installed by him entirely at his own expense. They were erected in the center of Fifth Avenue intersections, each tower manned by a policeman. He believed that traffic could be handled by light signals more effectively than by patrolmen on the street; that the public, taught to obey light signals implicitly, would soon come to realize that such a system was the very best protection, not only for pedestrians, but for all vehicular traffic. Policemen were spared for other work.

His method of handling traffic, at first doubted, even derided, has now spread around the world, and is used in practically every city, large and small, every town and hamlet. It would be impossible to estimate the time, life, and money which the Harriss system has saved for the world. Yet its creator, John A. Harriss, who is alone responsible for it, never made one

copper penny out of it. This was his outstanding gift
to his fellow men.

His main objective in life seemed to be to bring
pleasure to his friends. He needed no urging to enter-
tain lavishly, and caviar was served by the tubful as
well as the fanciest wines. At his dinners would be
found the heads of artistry, industry, and banking.

The doctor was fond of singing. It required but
little persuasion to induce him to favor his guests
with a selection on any occasion. It was not unusual
for him to join such distinguished guest artists as
Gigli, Scotti, or Nordica in a well-known aria, to the
tolerant amusement of the artist and the keen enjoyment of his friends. His untrained tenor voice made
up in volume what it lacked in cultivation. His favorite
selection was "Three o'Clock in the Morning."

To admire a piece of his beautiful china or his rare
silver would at once precipitate a gift of the article.
If a friend was arriving from abroad, the doctor
would be at the dock to meet him in order to expedite
the customs inspection. When he went abroad, the
police head of every city received him as if he were
a visiting potentate. If invited for a Sunday dinner to
the country place of a friend, he would arrive with a
profusion of choice wines and rare cordials.

He had the physical development of a Sandow, of
which he was very proud.

It was the sincere affection and implicit trust which he held for his friends that were to prove his undoing. William C. Durant had captured his imagination. He felt impelled to join in Durant's market operations, and he did so without evidence as to his interest or to serve as his protection. When Durant's second crash came and his great fortune melted overnight, it was found that Harriss was inextricably involved. His accounts could not be separated from Durant's, therefore his fortune disappeared with the Durant fortune.

Then, voluntarily, some of his devoted friends with large means came forward and contributed a sizable fund to assist him. This they placed in my hands, to be dispersed as sparingly as possible. Harriss would invent almost any excuse to increase the amounts which I was willing to let him have. He would allow himself to be sued in order to present to me the necessity for payment of the amount he desired. He never relaxed in his efforts to increase the allowance. Little by little, everything he had was sacrificed, for he could not change his habits.

Open-handed as the little doctor was with his own purse, he found it most difficult to ask favors of others. But there was one incident in his life which gave him a most welcome and providential surprise.

One day, while Durant was still head of the great General Motors Company, he and the doctor were seated in Durant's office. Pointing to a square block across the street, Durant said he would like to acquire that property for General Motors. The doctor said he would be happy to get it for them. Durant said that if the doctor would put up a fine building on the plot, the General Motors Company would then take it over, but that he himself could not bother with any of the details. Nothing was said about the cost or about any binding agreement. At that time both men had such large means that these formalities were deemed unnecessary.

The doctor got busy at once. The owner of the ground would not sell, but gave him a ground lease for a long term at a stiff rental. The doctor then hired an architect to draw up the plans for a skyscraper, and gave the construction contract to an outstanding building concern, all in his own name. He executed large bonds for completion, and the work proceeded. Then the second Durant debacle occurred. Both men were wiped out almost in an instant. The doctor's millions were a thing of the past. As he was no longer able to pay the contractor, the building operation closed down; as he could no longer pay the ground rent, the landlord was impatient to oust him from possession, which involved not only the complete loss of the partial structure but possibly also a large claim for unpaid back rent. The surety companies, being pressed on their bonds, became most exigent, threatening devastation suits. From all sides the doctor was deluged with demands which he could not meet and with threats which spelled utter ruin for him; all for trying to do a favor for a friend. Durant, no longer the dominant spirit of the General Motors Company, could not help him. The doctor stood not only to lose his entire investment in the half-finished building, but he was also faced with the possibility of large judgments on his unperformed agreements.

He asked me to go with him to see John J. Raskob, then an important figure in the General Motors Company, with whom he was acquainted. Raskob listened to the story and then he brought in Pierre Du Pont to hear it. They asked the doctor how much it would cost to complete the building and the amount he wished for his investment. Without a moment's hesitation the doctor said that he would ascertain the cost of completion, that he would be happy to get back only what he had put into the project, as he wished no profit— indeed had never intended to make a profit, having acted merely as a friend of Durant. He estimated that his own investment was about a million dollars, all of which they might check. They promised to give the matter prompt consideration.

In a few days, after checking the details furnished them, they agreed to take over the building, and also to pay to the doctor the amount of his investment, which he had stated to be a million. I suggested that it would be better for the doctor to receive his money at the rate of $50,000 a year for twenty years. I had good reason to fear that if any such sum as a million dollars were placed at the doctor's disposal, it was likely to vanish in a twinkling. The transaction was consummated in this manner.

The building is now known as the General Motors Building, still serving as the New York offices of the General Motors Company. After the agreement was made for taking over the building and before the matter was closed, the doctor told me there were debts of some $100,000 which he had incurred for money that he had spent on the building and which he had not included in his statement. I told him that it was too late to attempt to change the agreement which had been drawn up and signed, and that a request to do so might subject him to misconstruction and possibly to suspicion.

In view of the unprecedented magnanimity of Messrs. Raskob and Du Pont, I advised him not to disturb the written agreement, but to take the loss in silence. It needed no argument to persuade him that this course was the only one which he could safely follow with dignity. I believe that if his statement of his invested funds had included the additional amount, it would have been paid to him quite as willingly as the stipulated million, and Messrs. Raskob and Du Pont were desirous of making good a debt of honor, with no intention of driving a bargain. This incident is fairly indicative of the doctor's carelessness about his own affairs and of his willingness to suffer a serious loss rather than admit to such carelessness.

But the doctor's annuity did not stay with him for the contemplated score of years. Soon he was obliged to cash it in, because of his increasing stringency. He never got over his gratitude to Messrs. Raskob and Du Pont for their acceptance of a loosely-evidenced responsibility in which they had no part. He regarded their action as a miracle from heaven. He only deplored that he was unable to preserve what had been so generously provided for him, fearing that its loss might be deemed ingratitude.

In the end he lived entirely on the harvest of those friendships which he had so generously sown. But cheerful and hopeful to the last, he was welcome everywhere.

There was a topic which the doctor would never discuss with anyone—his age. Those perennial pink cheeks, those clear, bright eyes and those intact ivory teeth, he attributed to the efficacy of daily exercise in water. This, he contended, was the panacea, claiming that one who indulged in such exercise regularly would never grow old, and that he himself was the best proof of his theory.

Today, no one knows any more about him than in his lifetime, but every one of his host of friends carries in his heart the cherished memory of one whose outstanding talent was for friendship, and to whom each feels that he owes a personal debt of affection. True, he was reckless and extravagant. But he spread happiness wherever he went. His source of wealth may have been an enigma but his generosity was no secret. Although not the builder of any charity foundation, his life itself was one of good will toward men. Hence, though his scope was limited and his activities unheralded, he is fairly entitled to be included in the category of departed philanthropists who loved others rather than himself.

ALFRED E. SMITH
(1873-1944)

In the first third of the century there appeared in New York City some remarkable political figures. Because of the innuendo attached to the designation of "politician," it would seem preferable to speak of them as men who were prominent in politics. None of them rose higher in the esteem and affection of his fellow men than Alfred E. Smith. Coming from the lowly districts of New York City, bred in the field of ward politics, he held one position after another, from ward leader to Governor, gaining power, recognition, and admiration as he went along. He finally became his party's choice for the presidency of the United States, nominated by Franklin D. Roosevelt as the "Happy Warrior."

During the early days Smith frequently called at our office to confer with Mr. Stanchfield. It was not long before I met him and was invited to participate in their conferences. These started when Smith was sheriff; they continued as long as Mr. Stanchfield lived, for their friendship was both intimate and affectionate. It seemed as though I had inherited some part of that intimacy, for Al Smith always called me by my first name and he asked me to call him "Al" rather than "Governor." Trusting his friends, he did not fear to give them his confidence. There was no phase of city, state, or national affairs which he would not discuss freely and fearlessly, or in which he was not expert.

"Al" Smith was proud of his humble origin. He liked to remind the public that he came from the "sidewalks" of New York. Warm-hearted, loyal, and scrupulously conscientious, he exemplified Cleveland's phrase that "a public office is a public trust." He was one member of Tammany Hall whose honesty and sense of responsibility could never be challenged.

While not a law graduate, no lawyer of his time knew more about the state government. Without pretense to oratory, he could sway any assemblage by his wit, his logic, and his persuasive common sense. He originated a phrase which has survived even to this day—"Let's look at the record." He feared nothing and no man. He was always willing to trust to the good sense of the public.

No charity made a futile appeal to him; no complication was insoluble for him. His was a life of service; whenever and wherever he was called, he answered the summons. In every job he made an outstanding record. He had a way of consulting with those in whom he had confidence and extracting from them whatever information he needed. As Governor of his State he made a proud figure. He was a pillar of his church.Without bigotry or bias, he was filled to the brim with human sympathy. Every man and every cause received from him a full and fair hearing, for he was truly interested in every human problem.

During his regime he probably issued more pardons and commutations of sentence than any other Governor of the state. He believed it to be the duty of an influential man freely to exert his influence for worthy causes. Partisan only so long as he believed it to be right, tolerant and liberal in his views, he was almost boyish in his pleasures and habits, never disdaining to indulge in the ordinary activities which appeal to the common man. But his sterling character and his high sense of justice shone out in everything he did.

Knowing all the byways and artifices of politics, he kept himself above reproach. He dealt with leaders and with bosses all his life, many the most insidious and most powerful; yet he never was swayed from the line of duty. He was the man who elected Franklin D. Roosevelt Governor of New York State.

Smith's devotion to principle was shown in 1932 at the outset of the agitation for the nomination of Franklin D. Roosevelt for his first term. At that time the Smith candidacy was not formally announced although there had been some open activity on his behalf. William G. McAdoo came to New York from California, with, as was generally understood, the support of Hearst and the Southern and Western influence. His purpose was to stop the Roosevelt movement. His avowed candidate was John Nance Garner.

McAdoo sought an alliance with Smith to whom he would swing his own, the Hearst, and the Garner delegates, hoping thus to enable Smith to receive the nomination. He chose to confide his plan to me, asking that it be laid before Smith. When informed of the plan, Smith flatly and angrily refused to meet McAdoo or even discuss the matter. His antagonism to Hearst, due to previous New York State battles, was deep-seated, and the memory of his brushes with McAdoo in previous conventions still rankled. If such an alliance was necessary to secure the presidential nomination, Smith declared he would have none of it. It is history that the ultimate swing to Roosevelt of the Hearst, McAdoo, and Garner delegates won the day for Roosevelt. Smith might possibly have had the prize had he been willing to pay the price; but he valued principle above power.

Greatly as he admired Roosevelt's courage and ability, he did not agree with all his "New Deal" policies. Openly and boldly he expressed his doubts and his misgivings. While no "jingo," he scorned the idea of the "Forgotten Man," declaring that the only forgotten man is he who forgets himself and is blind to his own capabilities. He said that in the United States no man was forgotten, for every man had his opportunity. So sincere was he that despite his party loyalty, he espoused the cause of Wendell Willkie and hoped for his election to the presidency.

This meant breaking away from many of his old associates and from many close friends; but Al Smith was adamant when he made up his mind. He was not afraid to "take a walk" from his party, when his party abandoned the policies in which he believed. Yet when President Roosevelt ran for re-election the first time, Smith, recognizing the popularity of the New Deal policies, forecasted his re-election, saying, "Nobody shoots Santa Claus before Christmas."

He had been a great friend and ardent admirer of James J. Walker; in fact it was the Smith backing which had been influential in bringing Walker to public notice and then to high public office. When Walker indulged in his reckless habits and in his riotous expenditures, Smith repeatedly cautioned him, doing his utmost to keep him under proper restraint. He was as tolerant with Walker as though Walker had been his son. Without criticizing him or reproving him for his indiscretions, Smith bore with him to the very end, only ceasing in his attempt to conserve Walker's ability when Walker had proven himself hopeless.

In his appointments Smith was careful to select only those whose competence he knew. Once selected, he refused to sway their activity. When his appointee, the able Robert Moses, was laying out Jones Beach, the improvement involved interfering with the private hunting preserve of an influential friend whose convenience Smith would have liked to serve. When asked if he would endeavor to alter the plans so as to spare this property, he promptly said: "Bob Moses knows what he is doing. When he does anything, he knows just what it means. I would not attempt to interfere with him. And let me tell you that if I tried, I would fail. Such is my respect for his ability and his fairness." Yet his appointee, Robert Moses, was a Republican, and there was rarely a more sincere Democrat than Al Smith.

On the list of New York's great Governors none ranks higher than Alfred E. Smith. A characteristic apocryphal story is told of his unsuccessful candidacy for President. Smith himself humorously repeated it to me with a cryptic smile. As Smith was a Roman Catholic, there was considerable religious prejudice against him. To this he would give no serious recognition, although he realized its harmful influence. When the returns were coming in, and when he saw that he was defeated, he said it was alleged that he called in his secretary and said: "Send this cable to His Holiness, The Pope. Address, The Vatican, Italy. Now the message: 'Unpack—Al Smith.' "

His humor was an unfailing weapon. He played the political game fairly, honestly, and according to the rules. We owe many of our greatest improvements and public privileges to him, but his true monument is in the hearts of his people.

The Honorable Winston S. Churchill has said of him: "He certainly was a man of the highest quality of brain and heart, who rose under the free institutions of America—as anyone has a right to do—from humble beginnings to high, long, and successful executive office." Coming from a Marlborough descent born in Blenheim Castle, this is a significant tribute. Mr. Churchill says further of him that "His devotion to his religion was the comfort and inspiration of his life and his many private virtues; the gaiety of nature and personal charm hung on this golden thread. He loved his fellow men and was capable of giving them the noblest forms of service and sacrifice. Long may his memory be cherished in the mighty city of which he was a shining and faithful son!"

Smith had an antipathy to the growth of government powers. Moreover, he believed that this country had attained its premier position through individual enterprise. He often stressed and labored this principle. Realizing that individuals should be restrained from overreaching and despotism, he believed that the future lay in the profit motive and in the opportunities thereby given to progress for the industrial benefits, which he thought only such an incentive could foster.

One incident in his career showed his generous understanding. He had become interested in the New York County Trust Company, an old, small, but established institution which catered to nearby merchants, not pretending to compete with the giant banks of New York City. One of the latter class, the New York Trust Company, in which the Morgan firm was interested, found that the similarity of names caused much confusion, and suggested to me that the Smith bank change its name. When I reported this to Smith, at first he was up in arms. But as he considered the reason for the suggestion he consented to change the name, with the crisp observation that while he fancied himself a good fighter, he had no desire to challenge Jack Dempsey.

He seemed to know instinctively what was right and what was wrong; what was helpful and what was harmful. He declared that the energetic American needed only encouragement and opportunity; that coddling and special benefits would serve only to break down self-reliance and to stifle initiative.

His "brown derby," his reference to the "radio," his frequent allusions to his "Fulton fish market" days, were all merely part of the popular picture of one who was a veritable hero to his people. When he moved among the great, he never lost touch with the humble. All felt that he was one of them, that they knew him intimately, and that he had a fellow feeling for them.

He was an uncompromising opponent of Prohibition, as he publicly declared on every possible occasion, even when such opposition was extremely unpopular. In his personal habits he was always temperate, his only indulgence being an occasional glass of beer. He had a deep and sincere sympathy for those confined in penal institutions. Every appeal to him in which he found any merit, stirred him into immediate activity. He often said that his most painful duty as Governor was to review and to pass on cases of capital punishment. He would read every word of the record, get all possible information, and would never permit an execution if he could find any tenable ground for its commutation.

Despite his defeats and the sharp differences as to his policies, he will always be remembered with affection and reverence as one of New York's outstanding

and best-beloved sons, of whom its people may justly
be proud. Al Smith inspired an emotional admiration
as did few other public men of his time.

His untimely death was mourned as a national
calamity, regardless of politics. His bravery in abjuring
partisanship when it no longer squared with his conscience won only admiration for his courage and independence.

Al Smith was one of the Tom Foley boys. Tom
Foley had the astonishing faculty for picking young
men of great promise for the political offices which,
as a powerful Tammany leader, he had at his disposal.
Al Smith was probably the happiest and ablest choice
he ever made.

With a desire to be fair to all and to avoid favoritism to any, with the faculty of analyzing every subject
with a clarity of expression which permitted of no
misunderstanding, he kept steadfastly toward his goal,
opposing with all his great power any seeming menace
from whatsoever quarter it might come, be it from
his associates or from his opponents.

Smith may have sprung from "the sidewalks of New
York," but he rose to the Olympus of its great citizens.

In his last years he served as the president of the
Empire State Building, an enviable position which
he owed to his friend and ardent admirer the late John
J. Raskob. In that capacity he was as active in solicit-

ing and caring for tenants as the humblest real estate agent. No prospect was too mighty or too lowly for his personal attention. A great part of his time he spent as would a district leader, doing favors for friends in whom he believed, giving advice and succor where he could.

He was the Lincoln of his day, obscure in origin but outstanding in performance. Like that great prototype, many of his aphorisms have become parables. As Judge Joseph Story once said of a great contemporary: "While he lived, he might be claimed with pride by his party; but now that he is dead, he belongs to his country."

JOHN PURROY MITCHEL
(1879-1918)

John Purroy Mitchel was one whom it was not difficult to know, for he was direct and self-revealing. He first came to public notice as Commissioner of Accounts of the City of New York. While serving in that office he ran into conflict with Mayor W. J. Gaynor, a testy old gentleman of undoubted ability and unquestionable honesty, but rather of the curmudgeon type. Despite Gaynor's animadversions, Mitchel was well able to hold his own, proving both that he "knew his stuff" and that neither political favor nor public criticism affected him in any manner.

As Commissioner he received splendid preparation for his job as Mayor. His only guide in his selection of his lieutenants was their ability. He had been recognized for his searching inquiries into municipal operations. Fearlessly and effectively, he had uncovered many irregularities. Forceful and eloquent, he dis-

played outstanding executive ability. With very little
spadework he had been nominated on an independent
Fusion ticket and elected Mayor. At once he gave the
people a feeling of relief and the satisfaction of good
government. His personality pervaded every department of the city. His splendid record was unimpeachable.

Mitchel furnished a remarkable contrast to his predecessor, Judge Gaynor. He ushered in an era of
growth and progress. No coterie or special class
swayed him. Disgruntled politicians continued to dis-
credit his administration; all these failed of effect
as soon as Mitchel exposed the facts. None was more
familiar with the details of city government in all its
functions, none better qualified to understand and
clarify any situation, and none more alert to judge
their proper operation. His youth and his candid sincerity won for him wide acclaim.

But he had made a capital mistake in that he had
clung to his unswerving belief in the intelligence and
loyalty of the citizenry of New York. Unwittingly, he
made himself the target for the political parties whom
he had "driven out of the Temple" of good government. The MacMonnies statue, "Civic Virtue," might
well be called his monument. With all his ability, even
in face of his fine performance, and despite his incomparable fitness for office, his ultimate debacle

proved to be a sad refutation of Al Smith's famous philosophy that "you cannot defeat a real candidate with no candidate"; for Mitchel was overwhelmingly defeated by an obscure Brooklynite whom the electorate of New York City had never before known or even heard of.

An example of the canards to which Mitchel was subjected is an incident which I witnessed during his campaign for re-election. I attended a huge meeting of colored citizens in Harlem. The room was literally packed to its capacity. People crowded the aisles and hung on the rafters. Standing in the rear just behind two colored gentlemen, I overheard one of them say: "I don't like that man Mitchel. He's too intimate with the Rockefellers and the Vanderbilts." To this the other replied: "That's nothing against him. If it wasn't a Rockefeller, it might be another fellow who might even have the same name. That don't mean anything!" But it did mean that Mitchel had been thoroughly tagged with snobbery.

However, it was Mitchel's refusal to consider the political angles which was his undoing. Although he was a disciple of the Democratic faith, he had the unqualified backing of such arch-Republicans as former President Theodore Roosevelt, former Attorney General Wickersham, and former Justice Charles E. Hughes, as well as of such Independents as the Citi-

zens Union and the City Club. To one untutored in
the workings of New York City politics, he seemed to
be invincible. It was his extreme faith in himself and
his associates which blinded him to the machinations
at work against him. His administration had starved
the professional leaders and had ousted the hungry
politicians. So they planned ingenious assaults on him
in quarters where he was least prepared.

Espousing the Federal Government's request for
certain State property at Governors Island for use in
World War I, he ran into stubborn opposition of the
State Senate, against whom he opened a spirited attack,
impugning its patriotism. The Senate summoned him
on a charge of contempt. With the aid of such able
counsel as Charles E. Hughes and George W. Wickersham, he escaped censure. But here he received a fore-
taste of the kind of trouble which was brewing against
him.

Mitchel's mistakes were largely those of youth. They
were mistakes of strategy rather than of administration. He felt himself safe in the belief that an honest administration with a corps of able lieutenants made him
immune to criticism. It was his high sense of duty
which made him, his political ingenousness which
destroyed him. He did not realize that the Tammany
crowd, whom he had driven from office, would not remain idle, but would be daily scheming to oust one

whom they saw as a dangerous enemy and usurper.

Inadvertently he gave them many openings. When he uncovered some unsatisfactory conditions in parochial schools and suggested their improvement he was painted as a religious renegade. When he found deplorable public school conditions, he espoused a system for better space utilization of school premises that had proven very satisfactory in Gary, Indiana, called the "Gary Plan." This was maliciously represented as a species of serfdom, because it bore the name of Judge Gary, the head of the United States Steel Corporation. However, there was not the slightest connection or basis for the charge, for the school was named after a progressive school in Gary, Indiana, where children were enabled to have an enriched program by changing classrooms for various subjects, so that while one group was using a classroom, another might be using the auditorium, gymnasium, swimming pool, or carpentry and electrical shops. In this way, twice as many children were accomodated and received manual training, as well as academic learning. Twice as many children could be taught in the same building by this flexible arrangement. In other words, it substituted for the theory of the same desk for each child all day, the more modern theory of permitting each child to circulate from room to room for various subjects while some other youngster occupied his desk.

The idea was objected to by people who maintained
it was Mr. Mitchel and his supporters' idea to make
slaves of the children by teaching them trades. Demonstrations against the plan were held throughout the
city, and it was this policy, now employed in many
schools, which did more than anything else to defeat
Mitchel on his second nomination. No move of Mitchel's escaped distortion and denunciation—to open
the doors so that Tammany might march back into
office.

His support by the foremost citizens and their huge
war chest proved fruitless. Mitchel's position worsened
constantly. The Tammany banner again floated aloft
over City Hall. Such was the effect of a political
organization working against a proud record.

In a roster of New York City Mayors, no name is
entitled to higher rank, and none deserving of more
respect, than that of John Purroy Mitchel. For him
the wages of unselfish service proved to be death.

When England and France sent over their outstanding citizens in appreciation of America's entry
into World War I, it was Mitchel who tendered them
a public reception and whose welcoming address
topped even their fine oratory in the exposition of
the principles and motives which induced America
to engage in that mortal conflict.

Every public address which Mitchel made as Mayor

brought honor to him and acclaim to the city. During his administration there was never a charge or even an insinuation of malpractice or dishonesty in the city government. The Police Force, the Fire Department, the Street Department, all were ably manned and effectively administered.

It seemed as though the City of New York, that Augean stable, so long infested with political officials whose sole objective was to feed at the public crib, was at last cleansed and purified. Even those who had been dismissed from their civic jobs could find no real ground for criticism. Hence, in retrospect, it may fairly be said that the Mitchel administration was the ideal discharge of the hardest, most intricate, and most delicate governmental job in the country. Nothing was done in secret. Every public act was exposed to the full light of day. It had indeed been many a year since the great metropolis could point with pride to such an administration. Accordingly, one may understand why it seemed beyond the realm of possibility that New Yorkers, who had enjoyed the benefits of such a splendid administration, could fail to appreciate the boon which had been accorded to them.

Little by little the partisans crept up on him. When he was spoken of for re-election, he was generally thought to be invincible. However, the opposition was grossly underestimated. Under the leadership of the Hearst press, a mighty insidious campaign was being fomented against him. Although he was a staunch Catholic he was painted as an enemy of his church. His various departments, all well manned, were subjected to continuous and persistent diatribes. Almost overnight the tide turned under the skillful attacks of Arthur Brisbane, which were inspired by William Randolph Hearst. In that campaign the late Emery R. Buckner and I left our respective offices to devote ourselves exclusively to the Mitchel campaign. Money and oratory were profusely contributed for him, but all in vain. Despite the expenditure of hundreds of thousands and the backing of the city's foremost citizens, nothing could stem the avalanche.

Shortly before he had been inducted by the city's prominent men to stand for re-election, he announced his decision not to run. He then approached me, asking my help in getting a dignified executive position. One of the most influential firms, Messrs. Guggenheim Brothers, became interested in him. At my suggestion they offered him a roving commission at $50,000 a year. Full of happiness and gratitude, he accepted the offer. Then his prominent political friends bore down upon him. They insisted that it was his duty to keep Tammany out of City Hall; that only he could do this. He could not resist that call of duty; finally, he consented to run, and he was obliged to beg his generous employers to release him from his promise, which they did. Then came bitter defeat. Broken and despondent, he came again to me to ascertain whether the job was still open. As a defeated candidate he feared that he might no longer be deemed an asset. But the offer was renewed, and again he became ecstatically happy. But his happiness was not to be long-lived. We had entered World War I, and duty again called; he would not ignore the call. He enlisted in the Air Corps, after getting a release from that employment which he so ardently desired.

Without means he prepared to go to war. That sympathetic firm, which had twice engaged his services and had twice released him, came forward, and, with a few friends, provided him with a large insurance policy payable to his wife and his mother in case of casualty.

In his short public service, which, however, included almost all his adult life, he made an enviable record as the youngest and one of the ablest executives ever to serve the city. As a mark of public respect, an aviation field on Long Island was named in his honor, and a monument was erected in his memory on Riverside Drive. Thus ended a career of great brilliance while it lasted and which gave promise of still greater achievement. A fine public servant had given his life for his country. But the name of John Purroy Mitchel has not been forgotten.

WILLIAM F. SHEEHAN
(1859-1917)

William F. Sheehan, a full-blooded Irishman, came from Buffalo to New York, having been a power in State politics during the regime of Governor Roswell Flower, whom he helped to elect. Through that connection he had acquired some very influential contacts in New York City when he practiced law there with Professor Charles A. Collin, of Cornell, under the name of Sheehan and Collin. Among their clients were the Brooklyn Rapid Transit Railroad Company, which controlled all the elevated lines in Brooklyn, and the great Brooklyn Edison Company, which had a monopoly of electric service in that borough.

Such influential capitalists as Anthony N. Brady of the Brooklyn Gas and Electric, and Thomas F. Ryan were Sheehan's stanch friends and constant backers. It was under his regime and from his office that Martin Littleton became one of the negligence trial lawyers for the Brooklyn Railroad System, in which work he acquired his reputation as a barrister.

Sheehan, in his day, wielded a most powerful influence in the Democratic politics of New York. That influence became national when he succeeded in nominating his friend Alton B. Parker for the presidency of the United States. On Parker's defeat he was taken into Sheehan's firm. Associated with that firm was also Judge Edward Hatch, who had been elected to the Supreme Court in an upper New York State county and who served for many years as a member of the Appellate Division of the Supreme Court of New York County. Hatch had begun his career as a blacksmith. At great personal sacrifice and with indomitable courage, he had developed into an outstanding lawyer. His long career on the Bench had brought him wide admiration and high esteem.

The firm was called Parker, Hatch, and Sheehan. For many years it was one of the most noted and successful in the city. While Parker and Hatch were often consulted for their wise counsel on questions of law and on the effect of decisions, they contributed but little to the financial earnings of the firm. It was Sheehan who was the business-getter, who brought in the opulent, influential clients. Although an able lawyer, Sheehan never once went to court, but successfully transacted a huge office business as Solicitor. He was a corporation lawyer, handling large estates, and was consulted by some of the most powerful industrialists of his day.

Later, Judge Parker went into business for himself, practically retiring from public office, and Sheehan took another outstanding jurist into his firm, Judge George L. Ingraham, who had been in the Appellate Division. Thus it will appear that Sheehan was always buttressed with the highest type of judicial authority, and consequently never at a loss in ascertaining the state of the law or the probable attitude of the courts on any legal question that might arise in his wide practice. His firm was an ideal combination of theory and practice, the judges furnishing the theory and Sheehan the practice.

William F. Sheehan was a typical product of his time, when political leaders were truly "bosses"; when they settled the slates for candidates, controlling the party funds about as they wished. It was under these early conditions that Sheehan acquired his dominance in the Democratic Party of the State, which he lost in the later era.

During his term as Lieutenant Governor he was probably the most powerful Democratic figure in the State. Governor Flower was an influential financier, who, like the Republican governor, Levi P. Morton, believed that the successful industrialists were the best and safest custodians of the public interests. To them were granted valuable franchises with opportunities for exploitation, which, while they often fattened private purses, did not always achieve the public objectives.

New York City had from time to time been ruled by that particular leader who then controlled the majority of the other City leaders. It might be Crocker, · or Sullivan, or Murphy, who was kept in power by his personal following, wielding that power to maintain himself. The organization was perpendicular. The district leader marshaled and controlled the voters in his district; the city or council leader controlled the district leaders, and he in turn was controlled by the state leader, among whom the New York City leaders were the most powerful, especially on the Democratic side. Judges, mayors, governors, and senators received their mandates from the top.

It was this pernicious system which the Direct Primary and the Popular Election of Senators were designed to abolish. Yet, despite the bright promise of these reforms, it would appear that only the machinery and not the result was changed. The nominee was not actually chosen by Convention delegates. He was selected in a private hotel room where a few influential leaders conferred, and where the boss, after listening to their suggestions, handed out a slate which they in turn carried back to the delegates who proceeded to take the prescribed action. It was here that Sheehan was most influential. He knew how to arouse and intensify a movement for the nomination of any candidate he favored. He also knew how to prevail upon his few conferees to accept his candidate and to send out the order controlling the nominating delegates who followed that order. Never did he manifest his powerful influence more cleverly than when the Legislature came to elect a United States Senator in 1913.

Sheehan, who had kept his following active and efficient, was an aspirant for the post. His only candidate was himself. He seemed to have the election already in his pocket. While he received many votes on each of many ballots, he could not command quite enough.

About 1912, a young Democratic Senator from Dutchess County, New York, as yet unknown, turned up in revolt—Franklin D. Roosevelt. Starting with a handful of followers, he became daily more recalcitrant. The contest reduced itself to a fight between Sheehan and Roosevelt. The latter by sheer force of character proved a stumbling block. He was fighting the Tammany boss. All the Sheehan cohorts were thrown into the fray. For months the struggle went on with the result hanging in the balance. Each side seemed to be "stymied." Sheehan had all the big city leaders behind him; likewise, the powerful financial magnates who regarded him as one of their fraternity. But this was not enough. Then the power of the public press was enlisted. The fight became an issue between the bosses and the public. People began to realize that, in the Sheehan candidacy, bossism was engaged in a death struggle. When every expedient failed to reconcile the opposing forces bossism made a last stand. It would withdraw Sheehan's candidacy if it might pick his successor.

The Roosevelt cohorts, realizing that by no chance could they muster sufficient votes to control, agreed to support such a candidate as met their approval. Various names were submitted, but each, they claimed, wore the collar of the boss. Finally, the city Democratic organization suggested a man who, though he had been Grand Sachem of Tammany Hall, and whose party alignment could not be mistaken, had made a fine record as an upstanding justice of the New York Supreme Court. Nothing could be said against his character or his integrity, although his past activities indicated no special qualifications for national affairs. After some deliberation, the opposition, convinced that this man, Judge James A. O'Gorman, was the best that it could hope to get, pledged its support, and Judge O'Gorman became a United States Senator from New York. This fight was the forerunner of the popular election of senators, for which the Seventeenth Constitutional Amendment was adopted in 1919. To Sheehan belongs the credit of bringing F. D. R. to the attention of the people.

While bossism was by no means dead, the Sheehan regime was ended. Sheehan retired from politics and formed his law firm to handle the greatest interests which espoused his cause. An able negotiator, a practical strategist, with a sharp commercial instinct, he won for his firm a prominent clientele. Sheehan himself was no mean practitioner. He was ingenious and resourceful. But for the obscure Roosevelt, of whose existence he was hardly aware until confronted by his uncompromising opposition, he would have been a United States Senator. He attributed his defeat to the change in the times, to a new "order" of which he was not a member. With his loss of political power went the cessation of all his interest in politics.

The senatorial fight became all the more important because it brought prominently before the people the character and the forcefulness of a new figure. This was in reality Roosevelt's debut before the nation as a political personage. With this as a beginning, he built up his own political following, such that, in the National Convention of 1928, which nominated Alfred E. Smith as the Democratic candidate for President, he was chosen to place "the Happy Warrior" in

nomination. It was Al Smith who in 1927 procured
Roosevelt's nomination for Governor of New York
State.

Sheehan personified "the Old Guard" who went to
defeat before an order of younger men. He did not
have the ability or the training to equip him for the
high post to which he had aspired. He had merely
the control of a political machine which he believed
was powerful enough to win. Had he been a Root or
even a Platt, the outcome might have been different.

Sheehan's wide activities in politics served to obscure
his attainments as a lawyer. As an ideal corporation
counsellor, versed in the intricacies of big business,
he well knew his way around in the complexities of
corporation law and practice. As a solicitor, of wide
experience and proven competence, and as a resourceful and skillful operator, he verily ranked among the
foremost. Notwithstanding all of his sharp political
battles, Sheehan always enjoyed a wide following.
Even his opponents had respect for him, for nobody
ever impugned his honesty or questioned his sincerity.

He was a bitter antagonist of the "Free Silver"
movement. He openly aligned himself against the
National Democratic Party when it espoused that
cause, and was said to have been responsible for Judge
Parker's refusal to run as a presidential candidate on
any platform that opposed the "Cross of Gold." In

truth, Sheehan was constitutionally opposed to reform.

He would have been out of place in the world of today, for he could not change either his nature or his ideals. However much the philosophy of the later days differed from his, he was honest in his beliefs, sincere in his principles, and patriotic according to his lights.

CHARLES S. WHITMAN
(1868-1947)

Charles S. Whitman, a young man from the Middle West, had a meteoric career in New York. Starting as a Police Magistrate, appointed by the Reform Mayor Strong, he promptly manifested ability and independence. He also learned much about practical politics. Shortly after the Jerome administration, he found himself elected District Attorney, with the Jerome record to emulate. Not the bold, aggressive reformer, not the stirring public exhorter that Jerome was, Whitman carefully mapped his course, believing that there were many situations which he could explore and correct, with personal credit. First he invited to his staff a few outstanding experts to do the trial work, which he was loath to undertake personally. But he alone planned and superintended the preliminary work. He came into office as an able reformer with a fine record which furnished the basis of that reputation. Having but few political ties, he was consequently regarded as a strong, incorruptible public-spirited incumbent. During his regime he watched every trial and every inquisition, so as to keep it steered on the course he laid out. When some financial scandals broke out, he plunged into them without fear or favor, and prominent heads began to fall, despite the eminent legal talent which came to their defense.

It was these financial scandals and in the diverse litigations resulting from them that our firm became active. Always unyielding as an opponent, he was nevertheless habitually amiable as an individual. His inquisitional duties never affected his personal courtesy. With him his word was as good as a written stipulation.

One day Rosenthal, a famous gambler, was murdered on the streets of New York City. This was the opportunity Whitman had been looking for. He took immediate charge. The four thugs who committed the crime were ascertained and quickly apprehended. The four "higher-ups," gamblers (among them Billiard-ball Rose and Bridgie Webber) who planned the killing were induced to "sing." The trail led to a policeman, Becker, the head of the Vice Squad, who had been undoubtedly collecting graft. His indictment, trial, and conviction went forward without delay. His eminent counsel, Bourke Cochrane, could not save

him. Becker's fight in the highest court proved ultimately unavailing. The Court of Appeals finally confirmed his conviction, after a second trial, by a vote
of six to one. Usually such a dissent in a capital case
meant a commutation of the death sentence to life imprisonment by the Governor. The defendant, Becker,
had one last appeal left—to the Governor.

Whitman, riding high on the success of his activities, had been elected Governor of the State. To him
the last appeal would finally be made. Many thought
that, having been the prosecutor, he might have
absented himself and allowed Lieutenant Governor
Shoneck to hear the appeal for clemency. But Governor Whitman claimed that his knowledge of the
case qualified him above all others to pass on the
appeal. He heard the appeal and promptly denied it.
The four murderers and the corrupt police officer
went to the electric chair. The four wealthy gamblers
turned state's evidence and went scot free through the
skillful strategy of their counsel, Max Steuer.

Yet the Governor lost none of his prestige. He
was re-elected. After his terms as Governor ended, he
entered practice in New York City. But he had tasted
of public life, and it had stirred his blood. He could
not put aside the temptation to re-enter it. Years later
he was nominated again for District Attorney of New
York County, only to face defeat. Then he settled

into private life, closing his long political career.

The importance of his activities and the career which they opened for him, as well as his praiseworthy discharge of every duty he assumed, made him an outstanding figure in his time.

Whitman proved himself more adroit as a politician than as a lawyer. While he was not attracted to private practice, having none of the infectious enthusiasm of Jerome, he was a man of cool judgment, with an accurate evaluation of the political factors in his work.

In his career, he had evinced high ideals and scrupulous performance, having proved a worthy official in every office he held. While an educated gentleman, with an ingratiating manner and an attractive personality, he lacked that magnetic spark which inspires leaders to great achievements. It was the citizens of New York City who gave him his eminence, and in them lay his power. While to them, in return, he rendered efficient praiseworthy service, their support of him was not enduring, for he lacked the faculty of making it so. He was one of those leaders, potent in their halcyon days, who survived his zenith, rising with brilliance, but, after a short period of intense radiation, passing into unrelieved obscurity.

For all his political acumen, Whitman overlooked the most effective political asset of his time—one which he well could have utilized to great advantage.

Our country was in the midst of the horrors of Prohibition. In New York City no political policy was
more unpopular. It was being openly flouted, daily
causing violence and crime. Had Governor Whitman
privately shown his opposition, making it a corner-
stone of his creed, he would have won over New York
City, the Democratic stronghold. But Prohibition was
a Republican doctrine, and Whitman believed it more
important to be regular than to be sincere. It was
New York City which had twice made him Governor.
It was the loss of the city's support which brought
about his political demise. By failing to espouse an
issue which might have been his for the asking, he forfeited his following where he had formerly been so
strong, and, with it, he lost the state organization of
which for so long he had been the head, thus bringing
about his downfall. It was his public respect and his
private disrespect toward Prohibition which proved
his undoing.

To follow a figure such as Jerome was no small
task; and yet, during his incumbency, he matched the
great predecessor in power, in integrity, in successful
prosecutions, and in the public's confidence. But his
proper place was in the local theater, not in the state-
wide or national stage. His real achievements were
truly notable in cleaning up a locality, not in framing
large political organizations. Although competent as

a Governor, he was more effective, more inspiring, and more appealing, as the local District Attorney, despite the fact that as such he was not a distinguished student of the law nor an outstanding courtroom advocate. As a District Attorney in those parlous days, he had the art of winning and holding public confidence. That art he seemed to have lost when he rose to higher office, where there were no corrupt financial practices to expose, no gamblers to exorcise, and no murderers to send to the chair. His effectiveness in the one capacity proved ineffective in the other. His brilliance in his special sphere passed into an eclipse with his elevation.

From humble beginnings he became a national figure. Though he was a Republican in a Democratic stronghold of New York City he became a beloved favorite. As Governor, he no longer had the privilege of becoming a familiar daily theme for comment and discussion. Lacking the dynamic attraction of Al Smith, and without the hypnotic spell of Franklin D. Roosevelt, he found his charm immunized as Governor. The laurels which he had won as District Attorney withered during the years he spent in Albany.

As Governor he was only a name, not the electrical personage which had endeared itself to New Yorkers when his activities as a local District Attorney were featured in the public press. His political roots were not deep enough to survive a long withdrawal from public notice. If, as Governor, he could have kept himself in the public eye, and continued those activities which had previously attracted so much public notice with such public praise, he might have been spared the realization that he was a hero of the past, but not of the present.

It might be thought that Whitman's two great mistakes as Governor were largely responsible for his passing. It was certainly a capital error for him to espouse the cause of Prohibition when in truth he was out of sympathy with it. Again he made a tactical mistake by sitting in judgment when the convicted Becker appealed for clemency.

Yet Whitman's incumbency was highly praiseworthy. His appointments were all careful, and were made with discriminating judgment. The measures which he espoused were all for the benefit of the State. His vetoes had the support of thinking people. His public appearances were dignified and highly creditable.

When he returned to private practice, he was submerged in the crowd. True, he gathered a very substantial clientele, but it was not in the field of his earlier activities. It does not appear that he ever undertook the defense in a criminal case, or even in an appeal from a conviction, despite the fact that he had been a most successful and effective prosecutor. He was neither conspicuous at the Trial Bar nor in the Appeal Courts. It seemed that he needed behind him the dominant authority of the city or of the state to display his talents. When this was withdrawn, he had no distinctive feature.

Whitman will be remembered not as a Governor of the State of New York, but as the able, fearless, effective District Attorney of New York County who cleaned up a local miasma and rescued a proud city from the sink of corruption. As a District Attorney he was a shining success; as a Governor he was just an honest incumbent. Yet for a time he was seriously looked upon as presidential timber.

OTTO H. KAHN
(1867-1934)

A young man in finance who came into prominence in the decades just past was Otto H. Kahn, reputed to have been a native of Frankfurt, Germany. As a youngster he had entered the employ of an important international banking firm, Messrs. Speyer and Company. Later he went into the Kuhn, Loeb and Company firm, soon to be a rival of the great Morgan banking firm, and became one of the leading members. He was an amiable companion, a genial host, a deeply devoted adherent of everything cultural, who always provided enjoyment and information for those who were so fortunate as to share his society.

For many years he was an ardent patron of art and literature, President of the Metropolitan Opera, and an effective participant in every praiseworthy public movement. Despite his ineradicable trace of a foreign accent, he became an accomplished English scholar.

His writings on financial and other subjects, always couched in polished English, proclaimed the attributes of a highly educated gentleman.

When E. H. Harriman was busy building his huge railroad empire, Kahn was at his side. To him the credit was given for many of those brilliant financial operations. I have seen Harriman's original letter to Kahn, in which Harriman was most profuse in his acknowledgements to Kahn for his service in acquiring the many railroad securities for Harriman, principally the Union Pacific, whose holdings in the securities of other roads are reputed to be more valuable than the railroad itself.

Kahn's firm became the acknowledged mentor of such other colossal organizations as the Pennsylvania Railroad, the Southern Pacific, and others. The effect of World War I on his firm was at first depressing. It had so many German connections, its personnel had been so largely Germanic, that the public was prone to suspect its sympathies. Kahn's unwavering loyalty to the country of his adoption and his active participation in every patriotic movement unmistakably established his patriotism. He earned and secured the respect and confidence of his competitors, as well as of his associates. Important industrial leaders and government executives frequently came to him for advice and guidance. It was to his unceasing and devoted efforts that his firm owes much of its prestige and public confidence.

In appearance Kahn was rather short and slight. His attire was the last word in good taste and refinement. With his deep voice expressing itself in the choicest language, he was in any assemblage a distinguished figure, despite his somewhat unimposing stature. But no matter how busy he might be, he always had time for art and music. Fully half of his daily office visitors were people who came to him, not to discuss finance but on missions concerning art, the drama, and music. When the New Theatre enterprise was launched to elevate the stage and to improve our current drama, he was said to have been one of its leading backers. Whenever an ambitious producer wished to present an outstanding performance, Kahn would be the sponsor whom he sought out.

Every ambitious singer or artist, and especially those from abroad, seemed to feel that Kahn had the "open sesame" to the Opera. As most of the aspirants were unable to qualify, their disappointment often led to resentment and personal hostility directed toward him. Had he firmly closed his door to all such candidates, he would have been spared many annoyances. But at heart, Kahn was very sympathetic. Nobody could appeal to him in vain in the name of art, particularly musicians.

His spontaneous generosity in lending a helping hand often caused him keen disappointment and even financial loss. It was not unusual for him to walk unsuspectingly into a dangerous situation by merely responding to a request, for he never questioned the motives or the objectives of those who came to him for help or for a favor. He seemed constitutionally incapable of doubt or of skepticism, for he was by nature disposed to believe in people rather than to withhold belief until their good faith had been proven.

This persistent optimism did not affect the accuracy of his business judgment. When he considered any banking problem, his keen mentality would unerringly reach the correct conclusion. As to outside ventures, due to his personal confidence in human nature, he voiced no regrets or excuses. He seemed neither to learn from them nor to wish to learn.

Kahn kept himself well informed as to the affairs of all his great clients. He knew the immense potentialities of our country, and how, by judicial financing, they might be developed. For years his firm had been one of the leaders in national finance, retained by the largest and most opulent clients. He was its worthy representative on every occasion.

He surrounded himself with all the beauty which his exquisite taste could assemble. His New York City and Long Island residences resembled the Baronial

castles of old. Yet nowhere was there any ostentation
or display. From his handwriting, like an engraved
script, to his attire, he was the acme of refinement
and good taste. Without jealousy or rivalry, he was
forever intent on proving both his loyalty and his
ability; so that he brought something valuable and
constructive to whatever he touched.

He had the Germanic trait of thoroughness. He
studied the minutiae as well as the major features of
his problems. In addition to this, he was an extremely
erudite person. He could discuss Kant as well as
Beethoven, Leonardo as well as John Stuart Mill. In
nothing was he a mere amateur, least of all in sensing
human relations and reactions. Broad-minded and
capable, industrious and loyal, he could not fail deeply
to impress those with whom he came in contact.

Innately, he was an artist. It was said that in earlier
years he had political aspirations, and that his first
idol was England. Be that as it may, when he became
an American citizen, he was an undiluted American,
who rose, on every occasion, to the responsibilities of
a privilege which he never ceased to cherish and to
deserve.

If he ever felt that his foreign origin was a handicap, his career certainly disproved this, because no
native American could have been more public spirited,
more generous in giving his talent and his support, or

more faithful to American ideals and objectives than he was.

In his profession as banker, no other man of his day was more successful. His manifold non-business activities had but little to do with money-making. That they were frequently unsuccessful financially did not disturb him. He did not indulge in the arts or music for money-making. For him they were merely a source of exquisite pleasure, for which he was quite willing to pay.

He became a substantial stockholder in a leading motion-picture company. He early foresaw the great importance of this new industry, considering it as a means for spreading intellectual enjoyment and for imparting wholesome education, even more than as a possibility for money-making. In this he was for a time not mistaken, but poor management and reckless speculation by the officials brought about the inevitable result. The concern in which he was interested failed to achieve either its educational or its financial objectives, for it foundered upon the rocks of maladministration. It may be fairly said that Kahn suffered no serious losses except in the activities which were beyond the scope of his business as a banker. His great financial ability, his thorough education in finance, and his ambitious plans in that field, placed him high on the roster of the leading national financiers.

He was sure that the great enterprise builders of America would successfully develop our country in their natural growth and by their assured success, and in that progress he did his part as a banker to facilitate the development. But as he saw his duty, it was to go far beyond this—to give an impetus to culture and refinement, to devote his fortune, his interest, and his fine intellect to the achievement of objectives which were nobler and more inspiring than the ordinary pursuit of money-making.

Without pretense or publicity, he performed his chosen tasks, ever alert to support any public movement which he deemed inspiring and elevating. Lending and making money was his trade, in which he was indeed proficient. But this was not his sole or his chief objective. With him wealth was but a means to an end, and he never disregarded that end.

With his eclectic tastes and his winning personality, he had few rivals for the objectives which he sought. His nature had many varied sides; he was a leading member of one of the greatest banking firms in the world, a dominant spirit of music in America, a collector of rare masterpieces of art, and a profound student of economics.

The country of his adoption was amply repaid for the advantages which it gave him, and of which he made such grateful use. Although he was aggressive about what he went after, one could not but admire his honest sincerity. The versatility of the man and the sincerity of his interests were as genuine as they were limitless. Under his guidance some of the most important financial operations of his period were carried to successful fruition. Many times the great Metropolitan Opera institution owed its salvation to his activities and his support.

Kahn's optimism in every situation was as contagious as it was heartening and sympathetic. Teeming with brilliant suggestions, his fervor and his confidence seemed unquenchable. He was truly a great and generous person who never failed to contribute his full quota in everything he undertook, asking for no other recognition beyond the opportunity to serve. He would have preferred to be remembered for his outside activities rather than for his brilliant record as a member of his illustrious banking firm; but he richly deserves grateful remembrance and sincere appreciation for both.

CHARLES HAYDEN
(1870-1937)

Prominent in the top financial group of his day was Charles Hayden, a personality *sui generis*. Hayden came to New York as a rather obscure stockbroker from Boston, and he formed the well-known brokerage firm of Hayden, Stone and Company. With a brilliant corporate mind and a passion for such new enterprises as he believed promising, he rose to power first in the field of copper mining. Many other enterprises later captured his interest. In all he took an active participation. He was a director of more boards than any other man in his time—as many as sixty at one time. As such he studied the company's activities minutely, so that no other director was more helpful or better informed. The stock brokerage business was, however, nearest his heart. He never lost his interest in it, always eager to earn commissions however small.

He was quick and sound in his judgment. With

confidence and courage he would embark upon any enterprise which met with his approbation. If he disagreed with its policies, he would boldly announce it to the management regardless of its prestige and power. Alert to see any point, uncompromising when he thought he was in the right, he was always willing to listen. He had an extraordinarily acquisitive mind, and a remarkable understanding of figures. For him, no task was too exhausting, no fight too strenuous, once he had entered into it.

Hayden trained and developed a host of able young men, both among his partners and among the enterprises in which he was interested. For all of these he was a constant inspiration. They learned at firsthand his thoroughness as well as his manner of approach to any question. But he had a strange philosophy with regard to the wealth of his lieutenants. He did not believe in their getting too rich too fast. He believed that in order to appreciate the value and the possibilities of wealth, one must amass it slowly. Therefore, one of the tenets to which he clung was that his associates should always be men of moderate means. If his firm needed large increases in capital, he would make the advance himself, always careful to assure himself a substantial rate of interest. One may doubt the wisdom of his policy, yet his outstanding success would seem to have justified it.

Hayden should not be judged as selfish because he alone of all his associates acquired a great fortune. None of those associates were ever permitted to be in need or in distress, although each must fully realize that his own salvation lay in the integrity of his work and in the intensity of his devotion. Hayden's respect for ability was unconcealed. While he was a strict taskmaster, he was always an appreciative one.

He believed implicitly in the advantages of judicious industrial combinations. He declared that wise leadership could be exercised over a wide basis; that an able mining engineer could build up a competent staff to run several operations as well as one; that joint operations gave each the benefit of helpful ideas and resulted in large savings. He was also an ardent advocate for the unification of the New York City subway and surface lines. As a director of the B.M.T., he spent years working on the details of the eventual unification; and his numerous suggestions were most helpful to the city and to the companies. Moreover, he was much more than a broker or a mining investor. He was a banker in the broadest sense of the term. On the Board of the Chase National Bank he was highly esteemed and attentively listened to. This great bank, having acquired the dormant Equitable Trust Company, was about to liquidate it when Hayden purchased the entire Equitable Trust Company stock.

Henceforth, as the sole owner, he ran the Trust Company as an adjunct to his firm.

He attributed his financial success to his keen interest in any promising enterprise. He would travel far and wide, anywhere in the world, to make a personal inspection. When he was quite old, and when aviation was by no means so safe as now, he flew to Africa and down the entire length of that continent simply to learn what was going on there.

His activities were by no means limited to copper and tractions. He was an enthusiastic believer in the future of the moving-picture industry. He foresaw the development of aviation and was one of the most influential directors of the Curtiss Wright Company; as such he had much to do with its growth and operation. Likewise, he acquired large quantities in diverse manufacturing companies, such as sugar, iron, trucks, and automobiles; indeed it would be difficult to name any major American industry in which he was not a substantial investor. And he studied each carefully, so that his views were frequently sought because of his keen judgement and his business acumen.

Hayden was rather short and portly, with a florid, round, smooth face, clear piercing blue eyes, and sparse blond hair. He never lost the trace of his Boston accent. Constantly in good humor, with an habitual simplicity of expression, he had an air of good-fellowship. Slow to anger, he was, nevertheless, capable of strong rage, and not afraid to fight. In his contests there were no personalities, only principles; and for these he was uncompromising. If he thought something amiss, he would go right to the top with his complaint. On one occasion, when associated in an operation with the Morgan banking firm, he found serious fault with certain of their activities. He went directly to the Morgan partners to whom he delivered a broadside in no uncertain terms. When they attempted to assuage him, he became the more intense, so that it took all Mr. Morrow's diplomacy to pacify him by an assurance that the proper steps would be promptly taken, as indeed they were.

Such candor and directness won for him respect and consideration in all quarters. His associates came to realize that "Charlie" Hayden did not complain unless he had something to complain about, and would not be satisfied until his grievance was redressed. With all his directness and independence, he made many friends, and all gladly greeted him as one who merited their trust and confidence. While constitutionally an optimist, he was not without a realistic appreciation of conditions and trends, for which he made due allowance. With his confidence in success, he overlooked no difficulties, sparing no pains for its attainment.

He was unassuming and retiring. He maintained no

elaborate establishments. A modest hotel apartment, a moderate-priced motorcar, ordinary, plain, business offices—those were the extent of his expenditures. He had successfully weathered panic after panic, many recessions and slumps. He had one boast that he would never sell out a customer. When the account had fairly recovered he might insist on its being closed, but he would not profit by his clients' distress. Hayden was not noteworthy for his known charities. He gave to many, inconspicuously and moderately, but on one occasion he rose to prominence. It was planned to build a splendid planetarium to stimulate interest in astronomy and kindred subjects. Hayden's name was on the list of possible donors. When he was approached by a member of the Morgan firm for a subscription, only a small amount had been subscribed. When told of the amount lacking to complete the fund he agreed to furnish it, providing the planetarium would bear his name.

Hayden was a keen businessman whose great fortune never dulled the fine edge of his inqusitive instinct. He enjoyed the game of making money, and his score of winnings was greater than any of his associates suspected. His store of gold actually piled up in a veritable mountain of wealth. When he came to think about its ultimate distribution, he was at a loss as to how it should be done. Even when he decided to leave it all to charity, he was unable to evolve a completely practical plan. He had been so busy figuring how to make money that he had had no time to determine the precise uses to which it should be put.

He left it to his trustees to decide. When his estate was at last disclosed, the financial world and the public generally came in for a great surprise: this abstemious bachelor had left his entire fortune of some fifty million dollars all for the development and welfare of American youth. True, he did not specify just how it should be employed, but his able trustees have seen well to that, for his foundation has become a national blessing.

Charles Hayden was a typical product of the financial world. Thoroughly reliable, an indefatigable worker, he made of his business a profession to which he was intensely faithful. He developed his own code and he observed it religiously. He never stepped outside his world of finance. He was a "shoemaker who stuck to his last." His ambition was to succeed in his profession. He realized that ambition. He had no time for art, literature, drama, or science, with the exception of his one venture in the Planetarium and the purchase of a single Fragonard painting at a public auction. But the fruits of all his untiring efforts, the rewards for his splendid industrial talents, all these he gave to his fellow men, not in small amounts, but by the magnificent gift of that fortune which he had so scrupulously, quietly, and carefully amassed.

His life was confined within narrow limits, but he enjoyed it to the full. Although a bachelor, he was nevertheless fond of the society of estimable ladies, among whom he had many admirers. One year after his death, his executors, pursuant to his private instructions, sent a substantial money legacy to each of his score of prominent lady friends, to whom he wished to give his personal remembrance quietly and without publicity.

He was in reality of the hermit type. Among the great number of persons who esteemed him sincerely and who considered him their friend there was never any individual with whom he had a truly close intimacy. He attended social affairs and was a welcome visitor to Newport, yet he was seldom a host. He visited yachts, but never owned one. Many a dinner he would grace with his presence and his charm, but he himself gave very few of his own. He chose his career with deliberation, apparently believing that for him it held all that he treasured most. Despite his enjoyment of refined society, his social indulgences were purely incidental to what he deemed the serious business of life. As he laid out his career, so he followed it. Rest and play had little lure for him. They were luxuries for which he had no great longing.

Beyond the satisfaction which he found in his business success, Charles Hayden must have enjoyed gratification in dreaming of the benefits which he wished to bring to the many who would be the recipients of his bounty. And although he denied himself much, his self-denial had really served to increase the measure of his charity. He indulged in golf but amateurishly. He understood markets and securities; they were his pleasure, but he never manipulated them. He enjoyed participation in management, was a skilled director, but never an official. With his shrewd judgment and keen foresight, he limited his activity to the giving of advice, never indulging in the actual operation of any of his corporations. Independent, intellectual, studious, and industrious, he knew how to evaluate the merits of others, how to forecast the success of young organizations, how to apprehend the trends of commerce, and how to protect himself against the vicissitudes of market fatalities. In short, Hayden was a keen judge of the abilities of others, and of the merits of any enterprise with which he was associated. His great fortune had been acquired by backing his judgment; once that judgment had been formed, he adhered to it through thick and thin.

In life Charles Hayden understood the intricate game of business and how to make it reward him for his fine service; in death he joined those immortals who gave the fruits of their efforts to the betterment of their fellowmen. The very volume of his testamentory generosity and the simplicity of his personal indulgences which, though inconspicuous, were never miserly, entitles him to be honored as a true philanthropist.

HENRY GOLDMAN
(1857-1937)

No list of important financiers would be complete without the name of Henry Goldman. He was a patron of the arts and for years the financial mentor of my closest friend, Lord Duveen. It was through that relationship that I met Goldman. I also had contacts with him while he was the head of his great banking firm, especially in its joint flotations of corporate issues with Messrs. Lehman Brothers for whom I acted as counsel on many occasions over a long period of time.

Every meeting with Goldman was inspiring, for the charm of his personality, his Spartan bravery, his optimism, as well as his powerful, incisive mentality, compelled admiration. His eyesight was rapidly failing, but with staunch heart and brimming energy he met that great disability without flinching, still grateful for those privileges of life which had been spared him. He was a sincere friend, a tireless worker, a profound

thinker, and a brilliant industrialist. Above all, he was
an ardent believer in America and in American enterprise.

As the head of a concern which bought and sold
commercial paper, he developed a new department
in the banking world. He discovered that the public
would invest its funds in commercial enterprises with
a proven earning power; that invested capital could
be represented by preferred shares with a fixed limited
return, which, because of its security and the sureness
of income, could be easily disposed of; but that the
earning power, in itself without tangible book value,
was the greatest of all assets and could be represented
by common shares which would have a ready market
based on prospect alone. When he undertook to offer
to the public the Woolworth shares and the Sears-
Roebuck shares on this basis, the entire capital investment was reflected in preferred stock, and only the
earning power stood behind the common stock. Both
stocks sold readily, bringing a large fortune to the
founders and excellent returns to the investors. The
earnings, as he foretold, soon enabled each company
to retire all its preferred stock and sent the value of
its common shares to values undreamed of.

He would tell an interesting story about the Sears-
Roebuck issue which reflected an illuminating sidelight
on Julius Rosenwald, its head. Goldman said that

his firm and his friends, Lehman Brothers, had offered the Sears-Roebuck stock to investors when he
was abroad. On his return, being highly gratified with
the success of that issue, his firm wired congratulations
to Rosenwald, asking whether he had another such
issue which they could handle, informing him that
every share of that issue had been greedily taken up
by the market and was daily advancing in price. Rosenwald replied that while he did not have another such
issue for sale, if the bankers wished to make more
money, they should buy back all the Sears-Roebuck
shares which they had sold. The history of that issue
has served to prove the wisdom of Rosenwald's reply;
for every share of that preferred stock was re-
deemed, and the common issue, which originally represented only prospective value, has multiplied through
the company's unprecedented success.

It was the elder Morgan who first employed this
plan in the United States Steel shares. But it was
Henry Goldman who applied it to such a variety of
private commercial and industrial companies that it is
now a recognized standard practice. By this method
he enabled the owners of a profitable business to
realize on its prospects in advance of its future performance; and so investors might participate in rich
future profits by purchasing shares on their promise
of realization, relying on the keen judgment and ac-

curate forecast of a farsighted banker. His approval of a corporate issue was the equivalent of a "Sterling" hall-mark. He introduced the public as a partner in those great national businesses on which he placed his seal of endorsement. Through him thousands of small investors were given those opportunities with an almost perfect score in making good his prescient forecast of success.

At the outbreak of World War I, Goldman, always an avowed admirer of German literature, science and banking, was suspected of being pro-German. But he was really anti-Russian rather than pro-German. It was his hatred of the Russian butchery of his helpless co-religionists by their horrible pogroms which turned him irreconcilably against Russia. He looked upon Russia as a nation of barbarians, to be checked and not to be assisted. If he were alive today he would surely feel that his Russian antagonism was only too truly justified.

Long before the Western world had reason to suspect the Russian designs or to fear Russian duplicity and barbarity, Henry Goldman was convinced that the Russians were the most fearsome enemies of the world, and that civilized people should have no traffic or sympathy with them whatsoever. He frequently said that any nation who would treat an innocent minority with such savage cruelty was an implacable enemy to civilization and culture, not to be tolerated in the society of enlightened peoples. In his heart his sympathies were always with the English; among them he had many close friends.

While we were at war, his patriotism as an American was unquestionable. Yet his original attitude was construed as German partisanship, causing severe comment. Because of this, at great personal sacrifice, he surrendered his leadership of his firm and went into practical retirement. But he still retained his directorship in his favorite companies, which had prospered under his financing. Despite his failing eyesight, he was a rich mine of resourcefulness for every company so fortunate as to retain his interest. No other man could more completely unravel the story of a prosaic balance sheet. Under his interpretation it became a vivid, thrilling romance.

He never mentioned his failing sight. On any other subject he would talk cheerfully and freely, especially on finance or art. He took a lively interest in people and affairs. His mind seemed to have grown more sensitive and more acute because of his affliction. From his general conversation and his broad interests one would never guess that those wide-awake eyes were dimmed.

Though he was unable to read statements and balance sheets, his retentive memory recorded accurately and indelibly the figures as he heard them read. His concentration was so intense that one reading sufficed for him to grasp them both in their detail and in their entirety. He developed an extraordinary ability to catch from the tone of voice what others might derive only from facial expressions or gestures. How much he might have missed no one could surmise; but from his seeming understanding, it would appear to have been very little, indeed.

Goldman left a brilliant record in the annals of finance. To his intellectual integrity and accurate foresight we are indebted for the strength and solidity of some of our proudest industrial and commercial institutions. A fine business intrigued him as did a fine work of art. He approached both with respect and admiration, and both he guarded with a care akin to affection.

Business to him was not merely mathematics; it was intriguing poetry. It was more than a game; it was a mission. It inspired him with dreams and visions of grand accomplishments. With the keen insight of an engineer, he could discern not only the opportunities but the pitfalls in the path of a great enterprise. He knew the potentialities of capital well employed and wisely administered, and he was a master in linking money and management together into a magnificent institution for economic development. He looked upon past achievements as a guarantee of future success, and character as the solid foundation on which success was built. Each of his favored concerns has a secure place in his heart.

Goldman was not only one of the ablest financiers of his time; he was also a devoted patron of art. In his quiet way, he acquired a remarkable collection of masterpieces and works of art. He chose only outstanding examples of the topmost masters. Though small in quantity, their quality was uniformly high. His interest lay especially in the Italian, the Flemish, and the Dutch.

When his eyesight failed completely, and he realized that his days were numbered, he went to his friend, Lord Duveen, and gave him first choice of the Italian pieces which he was willing to dispose of. It was like taking over another famous collection—his favorite operation. Duveen, thoroughly familiar with every piece, knew where they would fit, carefully planning their destination, and, as usual, his plans did not fail.

As a tribute to his artistic appreciation, his friend, Lord Duveen, had presented him on an anniversary with a Holbein miniature, knowing full well that with his failing sight he could not see its beauty, but must construct it in his imagination from what he was told about it. Yet nothing could have touched Goldman more deeply than this recognition of his devotion to art despite his failing sight. He seemed by some mysterious means to apprehend every line and tone of the masterpiece; it gave him genuine pleasure to talk about it just as though he could see it.

Goldman lived long enough to learn that a large number of his great Italian paintings and sculpture were assured of immortality in the distinguished company of the National Gallery in Washington. He derived infinite gratification from this recognition of their merit. They are: Fra Angelico's "Entombment"; Giotto's "Madonna and Child"; Bartolomeo Veneto's "Portrait of a Gentleman"; Gentile de Fabriani's "Madonna and Child"; Bernardo Daddi's "Madonna, Child and Saint"; Titian's "Alphonso d'Este and Laura"; Giorgione's and Titian's "Portrait of a Venetian Gentleman," as well as various sculptural masterpieces.

Goldman's generous human sympathy is demonstrated in the story of Yehudi Menuhin. When this young musical prodigy, son of poor immigrants, was brought to Goldman's notice, he realized that here was a potential master of the violin. He considered that the greatest inspiration for the young man would be the gift of a truly fine instrument. Accordingly, Goldman purchased a genuine Stradivarius, the nonpareil of violins, for him. This benefaction, known to few, indicates both the keen interest and the great sensibility of one who deemed it a privilege to recognize and assist a budding genius.

Goldman was a striking figure, of medium height, with a dome-shaped forehead, piercing dark eyes, and a brilliant mind always alert to listen and to learn. When he delivered himself of an opinion on any subject, it was terse, succinct, and positive, carrying conviction from its very earnestness. Without pretence or egotism, he was forceful and persuasive, yet generous and tolerant.

Characterizing Goldman's business career, his close and affectionate friend, the late Philip Lehman, whose banking firm jointly participated in many of the Goldman offerings, and whose intimate relationship, both personal and in business, specially qualified him to appraise Mr. Goldman's work, once wisely and wittily said of him: "Henry Goldman put the gold into Goldman-Sachs!"

DWIGHT W. MORROW
(1873-1931)
THOMAS COCHRAN
(1871-1936)

The financiers who came to the front following the first decade of the century were a very talented lot, each with a characteristic background, and each, in his way, met the problems of his time with signal success. In the outstanding Morgan banking firm were two young men, entirely different in nature, whose talents so dovetailed that together they formed an invincible team. They were Thomas Cochran, former bank president, and Dwight W. Morrow, a member of a prominent law firm, who became a distinguished banker as well as an adroit negotiator.

Morrow had a mind as nimble as a hare, a personality which, for all his diminutive stature and modesty of speech, was most effective in its appeal. Perfectly at home on any question of law or finance, he was a specialist in handling situations, laying out financial programs, and impressing the stamp of his extraordinary ability on everything he touched. When his firm had a knotty problem of whatever nature, Morrow was the surgeon called in for the solving. Maintaining the high ideals of his distinguished firm, he had a native tact which saved them from missteps in diplomacy.

The least imposing, he was by no means the least successful of his firm's long roster of able partners. Although he was disposed to be absent-minded, he was never wool-gathering where concentrated attention was necessary. On one occasion, when he was traveling by train, he could not find his ticket. Each time the conductor passed, he looked for it in vain, until finally he confessed that he must have lost it. The conductor treated the matter lightly, and said that he might take his time in finding it before his journey's end. To this Morrow is said to have replied, to the conductor's amazement: "That is very kind of you. But can you tell me where I am going?"

His small stature seemed to impel him at times to overcome the handicap. He felt that he must act up to the level of his fellows. Morrow had been the classmate and the intimate college friend of President Coolidge. During the Coolidge administration he was a frequent and welcome guest at the White House. Toward the end of Coolidge's administration he in-

duced Morrow to accept the post of Ambassador to
Mexico. He made a noteworthy contribution by im-
proving and clarifying our complicated relations with
that nation. While in service there, he became a nominee for United States Senator from New Jersey, but he
died before the election.

Morrow used to delight in telling of his early meeting with Calvin Coolidge. He said that as freshmen at
Amherst College they had met in a three-dollar-a-week
boarding house, but if there had been a cheaper one,
they would have met there. Despite Coolidge's staunch
confidence in his judgment and his integrity, Morrow
told me that he never once made an unsolicited suggestion to the President. When he had an idea which he
thought helpful he would withhold it until in the course
of a spontaneous discussion he would be questioned,
as he always was. He frequently commented upon
President Coolidge's reputation for taciturnity, saying
that while he did not know how the President acted
with others, with him he usually did most of the
talking.

An instance of Morrow's unselfish public service
was in the controversy among the heirs of the A. N.
Brady estate, in which I served as mediator at Morrow's
suggestion. Three Brady sisters had raised strenuous
objections as to the handling of funds of their father's
great estate by their two brothers and a prominent

trust company. Like all family quarrels, the contest waxed bitter and persistent. This resulted in considerable publicity unfavorable to the trust company administration, the repercussions of which indirectly reflected upon all trust companies. The controversy assumed such menacing proportions that Morrow, concerned about the good name of trust companies generally, came forward. Through his officers I was brought in, and I finally arranged a truce, on the assurance that all the many issues should be left to an arbitrator satisfactory to both sides. But when the parties came to choose the arbitrator they could find nobody mutually satisfactory except Morrow himself, whom I suggested. Reluctantly, he accepted the appointment. He chose his own accountant and he relegated me to do the spade work for him. He held but two hearings: when he began and when he finished. He was appalled to find more than threescore stubborn claims, each running into hundreds of thousands of dollars. Then Morrow hit upon a brilliant suggestion. The sisters should not be permanently linked to trustees of whom they disapproved; and the trustees should no longer serve beneficiaries whose confidence in them was gone. Hence the brothers and the trust company should resign, permitting the sisters to select their own trustees.

Each brother was entitled to a two percent trustees'

fee for years of work on a large, complicated estate of
some seventy million dollars. Morrow suggested that
the brothers should relinquish their fees if in turn the
sisters dropped all their claims. There could be no
reflection on either side, merely a generous gesture by
both. Under Morrow's persuasive offices, both sides
saw the fairness and the advantages of this adjustment.
Thus a very bitter and protracted litigation was settled
to the satisfaction of everyone concerned. Morrow had
done a fine public sevice for which his compensation
was nothing except personal satisfaction. Only a man
of his distinction, with his impeccable fairness, could
have achieved such a result; only one of his resourcefulness and ingenuity could have conceived the formula by which that result was possible. Except for the
parties themselves, few if any outsiders knew of this
signal service to the community.

His constant companion and joint operator was his
partner Thomas Cochran, who had first held minor
railroad positions, then had become an executive of a
prominent New York bank before he was called into
the Morgan banking firm. He was as tall as Morrow
was short. With a stern, granite-like face, he had a heart
as soft as a woman's. No man was more sympathetic
despite his seeming aloofness. His charm was the anti-
thesis of Morrow's, but just as strong and compelling.
His mind was keen and alert. He knew how to im-

press his clients by simple arguments and by the patient, careful use of figures. He did not assume to handle the intricacies which were Morrow's forte. The two together made an irresistible team. Moreover, Cochran was always unselfishly interested in anything which affected banks and banking, regardless of whether it appertained to his·own firm.

Cochran had unflinching courage. He believed that the greater the banking firm, the greater was its duty to safeguard the entire banking fraternity. He declared that by generous cooperation the bankers themselves could solve all their problems without government help. He was a man of open mind, free of prejudices, eager for friendship, with a broad tolerance for everything except animosities, and with great practical resources.

Between these two men there existed complete harmony and genuine understanding. They were bound together, not only by business ties and mutual respect, but by an affection which grew greater with the years. Some of the most important operations of their firm were conceived and successfully effectuated by their joint efforts. Cochran would invariably give the credit to Morrow, who would insist that it belonged to Cochran.

Toward rivals in their field they were generous and considerate, believing that there should never be antagonism and never any justification for overreaching or duress. Many a tight banking situation which had little or nothing to do with their firm was promptly relieved by them in the general interest without reward or even recognition. When Cochran was deprived of the cooperation of his partner, he went into a serious decline. He lost all interest in living. He drifted into a chronic melancholia which nothing could dispel and which ended only with the close of his life.

Cochran was a generous philanthropist. He donated liberally to the restoration of French monuments after World War I, and gave lavishly to Phillips Andover, which he had attended. Of his many private charities he never made mention.

Membership in the Morgan firm has never been a sinecure. It burns up energy fast. It has made many partners old before their time. But these two men considered it a high privilege and a solemn responsibility. In that service they gave not only the best but all of themselves. The people of our country, and even those in their own baliwick, had no adequate conception of their accomplishments nor of their unpublicized services to their fellowmen. Only those who knew them well, knew anything of their remarkable services. They were both loved and respected but not fully appreciated in their day.

These two men were always solicitous to protect the

name of their great firm. They well knew that the
Morgan name had become synonymous with Wall
Street, typifying the unpopular symbol of wealth. They
were careful to avoid anything which might suggest
the concentrated power of wealth or might be construed as an abuse of that power.

Morrow liked to tell of an incident which illustrated
his attitude of mind. When running for the United
States Senatorship, he made a speech in Monmouth
County, New Jersey, in which he said that he and his
wife had had a frank talk when he decided to go into
politics; that when he went to Mexico as Ambassador,
he told his wife that he would be painted as a Morgan
agent going there to fatten his firm's treasury; that
every public act of his would be distorted in some
quarters into a nefarious scheme; that when he became
a candidate for the Senate the canards would grow
worse and that she must be prepared for anything and
should be resolved to allow no attack to annoy her.
This was all very well, he said, and they had borne
all the attacks without a murmur. But now he had
just heard it said that his son-in-law, Lindbergh, had
not in fact flown to France. That, he said, was more
than he could stand, and he felt that he must break
his rule and publicly denounce the lie!

As Morrow and Cochran did so much work as a
team, one could not avoid sensing the contrast be-

tween them. Morrow was always the architect who framed the plans; Cochran the negotiator who executed them. Both were fine bankers, with a clear financial vision, sincerely believing in American enterprise, having neither fear nor doubt as to its future.

There was never an acute difference either between them or between them and their partners. Morrow did not believe in litigation; Cochran had neither patience nor tolerance with it. Each was a careful student of public relations, particularly as to the public reactions respecting the activities of their prominent firm. Neither of them would willingly act counter to the trend of the times as he understood it, believing in cooperation with existing conditions rather than in opposition to them. They had no tolerance with quick, sharp financial turns, nor with fanciful schemes for profits, nor, indeed, with anything which might impair public confidence. Concealments or false promises were foreign to their nature, to be eschewed regardless of the cost or the temptation of profit.

While Morrow was the ideal, theoretical banker, Cochran had the practical mind, which knew best how to handle people, how pleasantly to convert them to his way of thinking. It is doubtful whether the Morgan firm ever had two such active cooperative spirits. By earning honor and respect personally, they increased the honor and respect of their distinguished firm.

A typical instance of Cochran's sympathetic feeling
for reputable banking concerns was his generous service to the New York banking firm of A. B. Leach
and Company, in which activity I was privileged to
participate. That firm, having an honorable record,
suddenly found itself in extreme difficulty because of
the recession in market values of the lesser-known
municipal and county issues and in Public Service
securities, in which it had long enjoyed a wide and
substantial clientele. Various Eastern bankers with
which this firm had its regular contacts and with
whom the securities had been hypothecated suddenly
began calling the loans. In vain had that firm endeavored to take up its securities by moving the loans
to large banks and banking houses in New York
City; for all of these declined to go to its assistance,
owing to the peculiar general financial situation prev-
alent at that time.

As a last resort, I went to Cochran for help. He
said that this firm had enjoyed a very good record,
that it deserved assistance in its difficulties. He then
arranged an appointment for Leach and me to meet
at the New York Club. Samuel Insull, then an outstanding Public Service executive from Chicago, came
on to attend the meeting as Leach's close friend and
valued customer. At the meeting Cochran questioned
both Leach and Insull very closely, as he studied the

list of the municipal, county, and Public Service securities. When he had finished his investigation, he took me aside for a private conference in which he told me that the Leach concern, in his opinion, was amply solvent and should be saved. He said that he would place one of his ablest young partners in charge of the Leach firm at once if I would assist him; that he would protect it by telephoning each of the lending banks that he had done so, and asking each to continue its loans; and that any loans which he could not arrange thus to be carried, his firm would take over, but that he did not wish anyone to know of his readiness to take over the loans.

This program was put into affect the next morning. Arthur M. Anderson, of the Morgan firm, was placed in immediate charge of the Leach business. Not a single loan had to be taken over. Anderson did a fine job; and he did it in record time. The Leach firm was saved. For this signal service, Cochran refused to make any charge whatsoever.

In the spring of 1933, when the New York banking situation looked ominous, Cochran evinced his courage and his foresight. He favored a proposed merger of the Bank of the United States with two other strong banks. This would have prevented the failure of the Bank of the United States, and thus would have saved the loss of scores of millions of dollars. He considered that bank fully solvent if it could be quietly liquidated in regular course. Broderick agreed with him. But the dominant bankers of the city decided otherwise. Unfortunately, Cochran was unable to present his views by personal attendance at a night meeting held by all the leading bankers to consider the matter, else the decision might have been different.

Here again, Cochran was actuated by his *pro nobo publico* motive, not by any desire of profit for his firm. Subsequent events and the costly expense of the forced liquidation of the Bank of the United States fully confirmed his judgment.

An outstanding instance of Cochran's great ability was proven by his consummation of the sale of two million shares of the Chile Copper Company by the Guggenheims to the Anaconda Company, in which he was ably assisted by Dwight Morrow. It was Cochran's patient persistence and his remarkable ability in negotiation which finally achieved that fabulous deal to the complete satisfaction of all the interests concerned in it.

The firm of Morgan has produced many great figures, but none won from their fellows greater affection and respect than did Dwight Morrow and Thomas Cochran. They brought into their work a vital, human element, which not only registered high in the result, but also left a happy after-thought.

They were generous while they were constructive, needing neither to defend nor to apologize. They considered no bargain a good bargain unless it was good for all concerned. As an effective pair they were were as unsurpassable as they were unbeatable. To know them was a high privilege; to work with them was a real inspiration.

JAMES R. KEENE
(1838-1913)

With the vast industries of the nation pouring their securities into the maelstrom of a great market, of which the New York Stock Exchange was undoubtedly the chief, there developed adept, shrewd operators who specialized in the handling and marketing of securities, who, by ingenuity, became influential not only in the commerce of the nation, but also in effecting the fortunes of the public so largely a partner in these enterprises. These brokers seemed to toil not, nor spin, yet they played a very important role in commerce.

Outstanding among his kind was the veteran James R. Keene. At the close of his hectic career, after we had extricated him from vexatious litigation, he outlined to me many episodes of his romantic life, illustrating the details of his activities; without sparing himself for his own mistakes, he explained the impelling motives which activated him.

His story was not one of disappointment or of cha-
grin, but rather a calm retrospect of the times through
which he had lived and a resume of the lessons he had
learned in his experiences. He said that he originally
came from California as a young successful operator
in gold shares. For a half century he was looked upon
by the great and small as the cleverest and the most
reliable of Wall Street brokers. Whenever a large
amount of securities was to be bought or sold, he was
the one likely to be chosen for the job. His clients
were among the wealthiest in the nation. They all knew
that they could rely implicitly on his discretion and his
loyalty, and for many years he confined himself exclusively to the business of buying and selling for
others.

But in that difficult game of buying and selling securities, he finally became tired of playing only with
his client's chips. At last he decided to put in some of
his own, feeling confident that what he had done for
others he might quite as readily do for himself.

It was this change in his policy which led him into
a catastrophe. He organized a "pool" to acquire a
certain listed stock, the Columbus and Hocking, into
which he admitted some very substantial partners.
The market for the stock under the stimulation of
this operation rose in an ascending spiral. It was the

talk of the Street. There were huge profits on paper. Suddenly, Keene discovered that some of his partners were cashing in profits by their own individual opera- tions, riding on his market and selling to the "pool." The bottom dropped out; several brokerage firms failed. To complete the debacle, it appeared that one firm, Messrs. Herzfeld and Stern, through whom Keene did some trading, had on the last day sold many thou- sands of shares "short" for a "numbered account," which, by covering at the low prices of the day, had thereby reaped a quick profit of several hundred thou- sands of dollars.

This brokerage house disclaimed any knowledge of the owner of the "numbered" account. In their till lay the huge profits to which nobody made claim. Exami- nations in the bankruptcy of the failed concerns dis- closed but little salvage for the creditors of those who suffered from the "drop" and no information as to the identity of the "short" seller through this "num- bered" account.

Keene went to Paris and remained there in exile for years. Finally "Sol" Hanford of the prominent law firm of Coate, Hanford and Laroque, who had been Keene's personal attorney, consulted my firm as to the possibility of Keene's making such arrangements as would enable him to return home without meeting a flood of litigation. The situation was still very complicated. There were several trustees in bankruptcy for firms who had failed as the result of the catastrophe. But no litigation was pending against Keene. Nobody had found any basis for reaching the "numbered" account which still held its large profit intact. That account seemed to be immune from the reach of the trustees and it appeared futile to try to involve Keene as long as he remained in France.

This was the situation as explained to us by Hanford. He said that Keene was getting along in years, all his friends and relatives were in America, and he was very desirous of ending his exile. He would deeply appreciate it if we could work out some plan which would enable him to return home in order to satisfy the Trustees and thus relieve himself of the dangers of his situation. After a careful study, with the help of Hanford, and as the result of negotiations with the trustees, we finally arranged to turn over the anonymous fund which still rested in the till of the brokers, as a complete settlement, so that without further outlay Keene could accomplish the result for which he so ardently longed. He was then able to return home in peace, but also in retirement.

His cardinal mistake, made only once, lay in taking partners, in sharing confidences, and in operating for himself. When he abandoned his fundamental principle, he became an easy prey to his selfish co-venturers.

His rapid "turn-about-face" caused widespread wreckage, although it gave to his disloyal partners a dose of their own medicine. The catastrophe which followed did not spare him, and while it may be justifiably criticized, he always maintained that he did not ask anybody to buy his stock and was not responsible for the huge impetus which his operations gave to the market. The defection of his partners gave him, as he believed, the right to protect himself against them. If the public suffered, it was because they gambled on what they thought was a prospective profit.

Though many decades have passed, the name of James R. Keene is still reverently remembered. It still stands high on the roster of the great in Wall Street. Wall Street, in its time, has produced many great operators and many remarkable brokers who acted for others. As to the latter class, it may be truly said that it never produced as skillful, as effective, and as efficient a broker as James R. Keene.

Keene had a national reputation as one who indulged regally in the "sport of kings." He bred and raced the finest trotting horses. Wherever fine stock was fancied, he was well known. But with his decline in Wall Street this activity ceased. And what a decline that was! He had been the super-broker for every great interest having large blocks of securities to buy or to sell. He had been entrusted with their confidence and with their fortunes. Never had the suggestion been raised that he was unfaithful, negligent, or inexpert. He finished every job with an unimpeachable record. He would never, directly or indirectly, "trade" upon orders that were given to him but would scrupulously refrain from any activity other than the selling or buying for his client. There must have been countless occasions when, with a large order in hand, he might easily have taken a position for himself personally, and probably would have done this many times with the consent of his client; but he never availed himself of the opportunity, with or without such consent. He conceived it to be his job merely to carry out the orders of his great clients, content with the commissions he earned by so doing, without any attempt to reap a profit from the foreknowledge which he had of his client's operations. His word was sacrosanct; his performance was immaculate. And so he might well have continued had he not departed but once from his role as agent to indulge himself as a principal.

In his later years, he was wont to say that the career of a market operator, as distinguished from that of a mere broker, was the most uncertain and dangerous in the world. He firmly believed in market and exchanges as the safety valve and the wellspring of commerce. He thought them the source of the lifeblood of industry. But he did not believe that any individual, solely on his own, could foretell the gyrations of economic conditions or their ultimate effects on markets: from one who had exceptional opportunities for judgment, this would seem to be an observation worthy of careful consideration. He said that no operator should patronize his competitors. What he made as an agent, he lost as a principal.

Keene, in his way, was an artist and a pioneer. He demonstrated how the public could invest its funds in partnership with the captains of finance; how thousands of shares could be bought and sold without disturbing the market equilibrium; how myriads of securities could be distributed or gathered without a ripple. With the S.E.C. of today, his methods would probably be no longer feasible. In his time, it was not the legal restrictions with which he had to contend, but the horde of clever market operators, all waiting for a chance to thwart his operations, to checkmate him, or to profit by his activities. The utmost secrecy and the most skillful strategy were required, and in these he was unsurpassed.

In his heyday Keene was the enigma of Wall Street. Everyone knew that he was constantly conducting huge transactions, but no one knew for whom. It was a current legend that Keene's right hand did not know what his left hand was doing. He would freely utilize other brokers, either to buy or to sell; but none of them would know anything beyond his special order. Yet in record time Keene's job would be completed, and thousands of shares would have changed hands without any unusual incident. It was his mystery as well as his capability which won for him both respect and admiration.

His career would seem to prove that even the croupier at a gambling table cannot resist the temptation to engage in the hazard of the game. It was not that his judgment was faulty, nor his philosophy mistaken; only that he disregarded the supreme lesson of his life. He left a career wherein he was a master to attempt one in which he was a tyro. As an agent he was an outstanding success, but as a principal a dismal failure. He spoke of market-trading as a fight in the jungle, where the wariest, the shrewdest, and the boldest prevailed over the corpses of their adversaries. In his philosophizing there was no repining, no blame for anyone but himself, and no apparent regret except for his own grand mistake, which he deplored mainly for its cost to others. He said "that life owed him nothing." His reputation had been firmly established. It has remained intact despite his one great mistake.

ALLAN A. RYAN
(1903 -)

Another instance where a man of unusual ability with exceptional opportunities misconstrued the function of Wall Street, mistakenly believing that wealth could be acquired there more quickly and more easily by operating shares than by operating companies, was Allan A. Ryan. Not until he found himself catapulted into a life-and-death struggle did he enlist the services of my firm at the urging of his wife, who knew of Mr. Stanchfield's friendship with Ryan's distinguished father, Thomas Fortune Ryan. Reluctantly, Mr. Stanchfield accepted the case, principally because he thought it might please the father, although the estrangement between father and son was then general knowledge.

Allan was always open and frank with me. While I worked with him he had few secrets from me. In his day the father had dealt with the arch financial buccaneers of his time, riding with them when they

were riding high; ever watchful, he parted company
with them when it suited his purpose. His method
was to profit on stocks by "a long pull," counting on
a company's success which he contributed in large
measure to by the financing which he judiciously controlled and by his sage counsel. The son was more
impetuous and less provident. He would not wait for
the company to enrich his holdings; he wanted the
stock market to do that. The father was a farsighted
investor who made each of his investments pay him
handsomely; the son was at heart only a market operator. Each wagered on the future, the one on his company's operations, the other on his market operations.

The most injudicious act of the son's life was an
open quarrel with his father shortly after his mother's
death. She had been mentally ill for years and had
been magnificently cared for by the father. Within two
weeks after her death, the father remarried. The son
publicly denounced him in all the newspapers for this.
By this single act he burned all his bridges. He felt
that he did not need his father's help despite the fact
that his principal claim to notice was as the son of the
influential Thomas Fortune Ryan. His striking resemblance to his handsome, clear-eyed sire, more than
six feet in height, with a slender, erect figure, ended
there. He inherited none of the qualities by which
the farmer lad from Virginia, through his own shrewd-

ness and acquisitive talents, had accumulated banks, trust companies, the great Equitable Life Assurance Society, railroads, tobacco, oil and rubber companies, and other national manufacturing interests, and had even become a partner of King Leopold II of Belgium in the vast Congo properties.

The elder Ryan holdings were as "gilt-edged" as they were vast; for, with his wise direction and the powerful financial resources which he could swing, he was a potent factor for success, always with a personal profit. He usually acquired the founder's shares or a large interest on the "ground floor," which eventually brought him huge returns.

The younger Ryan did not contemplate such a career. His father had bought him a seat on the New York Stock Exchange, which initiated him into the world of speculation. Through some friends, largely because of the Ryan name, he became interested in the Stutz Motor Company, and began to accumulate large holdings of that stock. Running into some opposition in the "Street," he determined to catch the "shorts" by creating a "corner" in the shares.

The market price of the stock climbed rapidly. He purchased all the stock that was offered. The public thought he had maneuvered a very clever situation. He had the "shorts" at his mercy, among whom, it was rumored, but erroneously, was Charles M. Schwab, his father's friend and associate in Bethlehem Steel. The "shorts" were driven to settle on Allan Ryan's terms. Despite my advice, his terms of settlement were so severe that the "Street" never forgave him.

He found himself loaded with a plethora of shares but no market for them, and at a cost far more than their intrinsic value. To acquire the shares he had incurred huge debts on the stock as collateral, valued at their rising artificial figure. Then he could not liquidate, as his corner had completely destroyed the market for his collateral, which nobody wanted. The market value dropped as quickly as it had climbed. Before long his debts caught up with him and his resources were exhausted. The inevitable crash came; Allan Ryan was in the hands of his creditors, who took over his assets for what they could salvage. Allan was "down and out," with no sympathy and no help in sight from anyone. While the father was a great enterprise-builder, who carved out for himself one of the largest fortunes of the nation, his son had ended his spectacular career by one burst of artificial speculation. Like a rocket, he rose into the skies only to fall to earth with a thud.

His father never forgave him for filial insubordination. He cut him off in his will with only a pair of shirt studs, leaving Allan's share of that immense estate in trust for his children.

The pity was that Allan, alone of the many sons of this worthy father, gave the most promise for carrying on the giant interests. He had ability, personality, and determination, but he lacked the leavening quality of diplomacy. Despite his final realization that the breach with his father had deprived him of exceptional opportunities, he at no time indicated any desire to heal that breach, allowing it to frustrate what might have been a brilliant career.

Allan was not disturbed when he aroused the antagonism of the entire New York Stock Exchange. Opposition made him only the more set in his course. He had many strange characteristics which did not greatly interfere with his rise, but which in the end became the cause of his decline. He was intensely suspicious and developed secret antagonisms against those who disagreed with him, resulting in the loss of practically all his associates. The anger which he developed against those who might oppose him overcame every other emotion. He then believed that everybody was his enemy.

His prototype was not his wise father, but rather the great stock manipulators of the past, such as Jay Gould. But he had neither the means, the resources, nor the opportunities for intricate manipulation such as Gould had. He never once blamed himself for anything that happened to him. Indeed, it might fairly be said that when the world turned against him, he stoutly maintained that he was right and the world was wrong; that he would do the same thing over again if he had it to do.

The fact that his energetic father, from obscurity and meager means, had elevated himself to an unparalleled distinction of power and riches did not for a moment influence Allan in the course which he laid out for himself, and which he pursued despite the advice of many who had been his sincere friends and well-wishers. He had grandiose ideas, as did his father, of building an immense fortune, but his temper and his temperamental proclivities served to prevent their realization. Just as he had no self-reproach when he antagonized his father and was disinherited, so he had no self-reproach when he found himself but a "fallen idol."

His early success had made Allan a spoiled child of fortune. It had affected both the accuracy of his judgment and the due appreciation of the world in which he lived, for he condemned those who had been his admiring intimates. Whereas his father had built a massive structure, with a solid foundation that could withstand all the eventualities of fortune, Allan's structure turned out to be but a veritable "house of cards," demolished by the blast of an unfavorable wind.

It is difficult to appreciate the prestige of this young

man at the height of his career. While his differences
with his father were well known, still it was generally
suspected that his father was somehow backing him,
and that his dramatic moves were in some manner the
result of his father's influential connections. For a
while it was probably true that his father was not ill-
pleased by the son's seemingly clever exploits. Those
banks in which his father was dominant were extending the son very substantial credit lines, but always
upon adequate collateral, the same as would be extended to any other customer, for the father had no
wish to hurt or to prejudice his son. It was only when
the Stutz corner was closed and the "shorts" were at
Allan Ryan's mercy, did the public understand from
his hard terms of settlement that his father could have
had no part in the operation.

Allan's father was a great builder, with infinite
patience, who did not hesitate to back his judgement
with his means; he never bit off more than he could
chew; he never laid a trap for gamblers or investors;
he was content to go in early and to bide his time.

Allan was lured by speculative opportunities. With
him a quick turn was the consummation most to be
desired. Therefore, these two men who resembled
each other so much in their intellectual equipment and
in their courage and steadfastness, were entirely different in their theories about money-making.

Allan's Stutz operation had been badly conceived and recklessly carried on, else he would have forseen the inevitable aftermath. The truth was that the son's situation was much like Heinze's a decade before, when he made his settlement with the mining companies. Allan had stretched his resources to the absolute limit to carry through his Stutz "corner." He could look for no help from his rich father, nor did he seek any. All he could do was to "throw in the sponge."

The father could have prevented this debacle at the start; he could have successfully guided its progress; he could have saved it at the end. His impassive unconcern was the result of that unfortunate family controversy. Yet the father was an extremely religious and charitable man. He built churches; he contributed liberally to all worthy charities.

Allan's greatest mistake lay in failing to understand those qualities which had made his father a tremendous power. He saw only the results; he disregarded the mechanics. With his father the building of a fortune had been a science; with the son it was only a skillful speculation, in which his early success and the prestige of his name turned his head. He staked his all on the turn of the wheel and lost. He had the ability but he lacked the philosophy.

Finance to Allan Ryan was a game in which the winnings went to the cleverest player; to his father it was a profound study in which the rewards came from constructive planning and painstaking patient effort. The father looked to the distant future, the son to the immediate present. Each backed his judgment, the one with his keen business acumen, the other by adroit manipulation. The one built on solid rock, the other on shifting sands. In the face of economic disturbances, the father was unshaken, indeed able to gain by falling prices, whereas the son was completely destroyed.

Allan's willfulness and sense of grievance were not confined to his financial operations. He had a wonderful family of many sons and daughters, and a devoted wife who lived only for her family and husband. In the depth of his misfortunes, when he was convinced that the whole world was against him, he became alienated from practically all of his family, even from his wife. He finally went off on his own with little care or thought of those for whom he was responsible.

The elder Ryan did not visit upon the grandchildren the unforgiven grievance which he held against his son. He generously overlooked the fact that some of Allan's children, from purely affectionate motives, still clung to the father whom they adored. It is said that Allan's last years were made comfortable for him by the children sharing their inheritance with him; in the end he was not entirely deprived of his patrimony.

Allan was a striking victim of the fallacy that there is a short, easy road to wealth and power. He thought he could read and thereby foretell market trends, instead of analyzing and forecasting the economic development of industrial enterprises. It was the tape and not the balance sheet which guided him. For him the world was an oyster waiting only to be pried open that it might yield him its precious pearl. For his father it was a deep mine to be carefully tested, to be laboriously studied, and skillfully developed, to the end that its treasure might ultimately be won.

FRITZ AUGUSTUS HEINZE
(1864-1914)

One of the most engaging of mining operators early in the century was Fritz Augustus Heinze. It was at the desperate turn of his fortunes that he came to me. I had been vigorously pressing some substantial claims against him, yet I had never met him. One day Heinze called on me to propose that he would settle all those claims in full if I became his personal adviser.

He said that each successive Federal Grand Jury seemed to find new grounds for his indictment, that he had numerous lawyers but no one to pilot him through the surging sea of troubles which threatened to engulf him. Therefore, he wished to have one who would do nothing but study his personal situation. I frankly told him that I had had no experience whatever in criminal or financial controversies, but this did not seem to matter.

He said my fee was to be $5,000 to be paid quarterly,

the first installment to be paid at once, and he would settle all the claims which I then had against him. This was by far the best fee that I had been offered up to that time. And I felt that if he were willing to retain me despite my inexperience in the law involved, I should not hesitate to accept the offer. He put me to work with some of his employees, studying all the banking transactions which entered into his numerous indictments.

I began a detailed study of such laws which might be applied to his case. I made a complete, comprehensive digest of each similar case, thoroughly indexed, so that I could readily turn to it. This involved some months of intensive study, but proved to be helpful in his defense when the occasion arose.

While I felt myself competent to "brief" the lawyer who would try his case, I thought he should secure the services of an outstanding trial expert, a recognized leading barrister, to undertake that extremely difficult task. I conferred with such able attorneys as I happened to know in the criminal trial field, in order to ascertain the name of an experienced counsel whom Heinze could retain. I went to see Howard S. Gans, who had been in charge, under District Attorney Jerome himself. Both of these recommended John B. Stanchfield as the ablest person to handle the case. I had heard of Mr. Stanchfield. I knew that he was one of the leading trial lawyers of the country, and that he had recently come to New York to devote himself exclusively to trial work. Gans introduced me to Mr. Stanchfield.

When I suggested to Mr. Stanchfield that he take Heinze's case, he said that he was free to serve, but he feared that Heinze would prove to be a difficult client. He had heard that Heinze was an extremely belligerent man who had been spoilt by his early success in the West, and he might be hard to manage in a serious case. He further said that he knew that there was intense antagonism to Heinze in New York City, and that his erstwhile association with Charles W. Morse, a convicted bank operator, would undoubtedly militate against him. But, he said, Heinze might well be proven innocent, even though his former associate had been proven guilty. He finally said he would accept the retainer, but that as he had only a small office with no assistants, he was not equipped to prepare the case and would be obliged to rely upon me for preparation. This would involve intense work for many months with frequent conferences between us, so that I would have to work even harder than he, in order to enable him to do justice to Heinze's cause.

There followed a year of close cooperation with Mr. Stanchfield, with almost daily conferences. This

developed, at the conclusion of the Heinze case, into
a partnership that continued all the rest of Mr.
Stanchfield's life.

Heinze came from a well-to-do New York family.
He had had a good technical education. He also had
a soaring ambition, unusual physical energy, a winning
personality, and an irresistible charm. Fresh from
college, he had gone West into the stirring mining
communities of Montaina, Idaho and Utah, to seek
his fortune. His early career was truly an adven-
turer's romance.

He plunged into the wilds of an undeveloped
country, where the law of the jungle still seemed to
prevail, and met the rough, untutored denizens on their
own grounds. He would fraternize with them, join in
their carousals, sympathize with their antagonisms
toward the overlords, and enlist with them in grandiose plans to improve their conditions and to share
what could be picked up through their help and his
ingenuity.

It was his opinion, after a little investigation, that
the current mining methods were wasteful and unscien-
tific. He believed that the large operating companies
were discarding quantities of low-grade ore from
which he could make a profitable recovery. He felt that
fortunes lay in what others had discarded. With his
associates he succeeded in raising small funds to buy

some of the ore deposits. He promptly proved the soundness of his theory. It also made the large operators suspicious of him and his associates.

He soon learned the quirks and intricacies of current mining laws. He knew that litigation was a foe which the large companies abhorred and would pay handsomely to avoid. Attracting friends and partners quickly, he surrounded himself with free-lance engineers and bold prospectors, through whom he embarked upon various operations, usually profitable. In his following were not only miners and prospectors, but voters as well. They were all useful not only for their leads and information but also for the support they could elicit from the lower classes. Hence, Heinze became their idol and their leader.

He evolved a plan to fight the powerful mining companies, who were none too popular with the working classes, both in the field and in the courts. This led to local brawls and bitter controversies, landing Heinze eventually in the courts, which in those days were run by mass politics. Cases were decided at the polls rather than in the courtroom.

Before his smug adversaries knew it, "F. A." (as he was affectionately known by his crew) had become a power in this region of rich ore reserves and discarded pay dumps. He elected mayors, congressmen, judges, and peace officers. He staked claims as he wished, regardless of whether they infringed on those of the giant operators. Whatever he did, he had the support of the crowd. He filled the court with litigations and the mines with riots. It is said that when at the end of one of his important cases his adversary asked the court for time to submit a brief, the court responded: "You may have until next Tuesday to prepare your brief, and on Wednesday I shall decide the case for Mr. Heinze!"

While all this drained his meager resources, he preempted such funds as he could muster from his associates, until suddenly the overlords began to recognize that they were facing a major threat. What they did not know was that he had nearly exhausted his means in the fight. They decided to settle with him just at the time when he was financially beaten. Then it was that he came back East to catch his breath and to secure new funds for mining exploitation.

This was the mistake of his life. He walked into the lion's den without even realizing that he was taking on the king of beasts! He left the mining rabble, where he was at home, for the gentlemen bankers, where he was a stranger. He took a seat in a game which he did not understand, an easy victim for the experts. One such expert, Charles W. Morse, was then riding high in the New York City banking world. The Street rang with his achievements. He acquired bank

after bank and he went after Heinze. He finally landed
him in a bank, The Mercantile National, which Heinze
bought, mostly on credit, from the Edwin Gould interests and Heinze became its president. It took all of
Heinze's ready cash, and very much more, to buy the
necessary shares. He was never able to pay in full his
obligations for their purchase.

Then came the panic of 1907, and Heinze found himself and his bank in serious trouble. His banking mentor, Morse, had "come a cropper" and was sent to
Atlanta. Heinze was facing a similar fate. The federal
district attorney decided to seize the books of the
Heinze companies, who had been heavy borrowers
from the Heinze bank. None of the Heinze attorneys
had any knowledge of the location of the Heinze books
and records. Whatever had been done with them
only Heinze knew. Then started a chase which led back
and forth across the continent, from New York to
Montana, then to Idaho and Utah, and then back to
New York. Mr. Stanchfield bitterly deplored the incident as prejudicing Heinze's chances on his impending
trial. The Government finally caught up with a Heinze
minion in a New York boarding house. With him was
a large, heavy trunk which was thought to contain the
desired records. When it was opened, it held only old
newspapers. No one ever discovered what had become
of the books or how they had been spirited away.

The Government was next on the track of some other desired records of a Heinze concern, the Ohio Copper Company, which had been in the possession of that company's president in New York. All the directors were served with *subpoenas,* but not until all had resigned in protest against these tactics and their successors had been elected. The president had secretly taken the books with him to his hotel in Spring Lake, New Jersey, where they disappeared in a fire which destroyed the hotel and its contents. Heinze and the president were both indicted, but that indictment never came to trial.

In such unfavorable circumstances, and the inevitable attendant publicity, the Heinze bank indictment came to trial before Judge Hough, the same judge who had sent Morse to jail for fifteen years. The Heinze trial aroused nationwide interest. During it, Mr. Stanchfield through his ultimate victory, made a national reputation as the attorney for the defense. In the course of that trial he told Heinze that he would not place him on the stand, as the disappearance of the books would prove an insuperable handicap. Heinze protested vigorously, saying that he had been a witness in scores of trials and had never been upset. To this Mr. Stanchfield calmly replied: "Well, Fritz Heinze, if you go into that witness box you may find yourself in Atlanta breaking stones. If you keep away from it, I may win your case

for you." That ended the argument. Mr. Stanchfield
made good his promise, although it took several years
of fierce litigation to do so.

Extricated from the meshes of the law, Heinze
endeavored in vain to recoup himself in the stock
market. But that was not his metier. There he fought
against overwhelming odds. He resorted to every manner of stock manipulation, but to no avail. Those whom
he had vanquished in the West had him at their mercy
in the East. His companies, none too strong at best,
foundered one by one, dying from inanition. Fritz
Heinze soon became a man with a past but no future.
Although endowed with an unusual ability to appraise
and to operate mining properties, he had grown too
fast. He had become too powerful in his own bailiwick.
He proceeded to fritter away his small remaining
resources and to dissipate his strength in unwise
living. He quickly passed into oblivion. But his
Western fights are not forgotten.

Fritz Heinze was a daredevil at heart. He regarded
the market as a place to raise money, but he was not too
careful in the promises made or the prospects which he
evaluated. In that time there was no R.F.C. or Government regulation to safeguard investors. The general
principle in vogue was *caveat emptor*. The public,
always eager to gamble, looked upon Heinze as a great
mining engineer of startling achievements. But Heinze

was not acquainted with the possibilities of the "Bear" activity. He did not realize, until it was too late, that the "shorts" could ruin any concern by long-sustained and relentless activity. He considered himself to be a "Little Napoleon," but he disregarded that gentleman's misfortunes after he went into Russia.

Heinze was soon only a memory. Careless overindulgence and habitual imprudence soon finished him, bringing him to an early grave. But he certainly was a bright star at his zenith. Had he adhered to his proper objectives, in his own field, he would have undoubtedly achieved an outstanding success.

He had the ability, the industry, the resourcefulness, and the courage of those early adventurers who opened up the great West by bringing its hidden treasures into the service of mankind. Moreover, he had the vision, too; but he mistakenly assumed that there was an easier way to wealth than prospecting and developing mines. That he was a man of great force, with an appealing and impressive personality, cannot be denied. Even his enemies had personal admiration for him though they loudly denounced his methods.

WALTER P. CHRYSLER
(1875-1940)

One day in the early twenties, as I was intently engaged on some papers, the office boy brought me a slip
bearing the name of Mr. Chrysler. It was a name un-
familiar to me, and, as he pronounced it, I thought at
once of Fritz Kreisler, the famous violinist. I asked
the boy whether he had spelt the name correctly. He
replied that the visitor had spelt it himself. In a few
moments the man opened my door. I shall never forget
my first impression of him. He was a rather stocky man,
with a narrow, pointed, smooth-shaven face, a long,
slender, aquiline nose, a high forehead, and piercing
dark eyes. His was a face which one would not forget.

He began to talk rapidly with a curious Midwestern
twang which was difficult for me to understand. I made
out, however, that "Billy" had sent him to me, from
which, as he talked about an automobile manufacturer,

I gleamed that he meant William C. "Billy" Durant.

His attire was as strange as his manner of speaking. He wore a light plaid suit, a dark-toned shirt, with a gaily-colored tie in which was inserted, as I recall, a sizeable diamond pin. Although his name meant nothing to me, I was impressed with the fact that here was a very remarkable person. As I induced him to tell me more about himself, I became amazed at his story. He took out of his inside breast pocket a somewhat worn and soiled sheaf of papers. He said that he had read them but did not understand them. As I proceeded to read them, my amazement grew still greater, until I could hardly believe my eyes. While I was reading, he sat there quietly answering my occasional questions.

I gathered, after a quick perusal of his complicated papers, that he had been the head of the Buick Company, and that this company, in consideration of the termination of his contract before its expiration, had given him certain advantages as the price of the termination in the nature of "severance pay." As these advantages seemed to me extraordinarily large, I asked him to tell me what his work had been, what he had accomplished for the firm, and why he was given such substantial "severance pay." He then proceeded in his own way to narrate in some detail his origin, his efforts, and his activities; from which there emerged the fantastic tale which is here reported with careful fidelity to the facts as he gave them to me.

His story is one of a humble mechanic whose imagination was stirred by the magic of an engine. Born of German stock in a small Kansas town, and the son of a locomotive engineer, he had started as a sweeper in an engine house, working ten hours a day for a dollar. After a few months he progressed to the position of apprentice in the Union Pacific shop. There he began to study tools, which became the passion of his life. He went from one railroad job to another, always advancing in his shop positions, at meager salaries, but learning all the way, until there was nothing he could not do with or on a locomotive. In his early teens he had made every part of a model locomotive, had assembled them, and had run the completed machine on a toy track which he had built in his backyard. Having become generally known in the industry as an expert master locomotive mechanic, he left railroading for manufacturing. He was hired by the American Locomotive Company as superintendent of its Allegheny shop.

In 1918, he had gone to Chicago to visit an automobile show where he had fallen in love with a Locomobile touring car, the price of which was $5,000. Although he had only $700, he managed to wangle a loan for the balance and brought the car home, not to ride in, but to study. Putting it into his barn, he worked on it night after night, examining every part and gadget, taking it apart, and putting it together again. Over and over he studied its every function, until he knew it as well as he knew the locomotive. Feeling the lack of technical education, he had been devotedly pursuing correspondence courses for seven years, so that he could now hold his own even with college trained engineers. In practical knowledge he towered above them by reason of what he had acquired with his eyes and hands. Then, suddenly, he was summoned by a New York banker, who was a director of the American Locomotive Company and of the General Motors Company. When asked by the banker whether he had given any thought to automobile manufacturing, he replied: "Yes, sir! I have been thinking about it for four or five years." He was invited to join the Buick Company at Flint, Michigan. The president, Charles W. Nash, gave him the job of remodeling the shop at a salary of $6,000 year—just half of what he had been getting.

Things began to hum. New methods were installed, labor-saving devices were employed, costs went down, and production went up. It was in the year of his entrance into that field that Charles F. Kettering, an inventive engineering genius came to the front, ultimately to join General Motors, and his remarkable inventions gave a powerful stimulus to the whole industry.

From a production of forty-five cars a day, Chrysler rapidly reached two hundred cars per day. After three years as work manager at the Buick factory, Chrysler suddenly announced to Nash that he wished to receive a salary of $25,000 a year. Dumfounded, Nash called in the New York banker who had given Chrysler his job. Chrysler got his raise. He was then forty years old.

It was at that time that William Durant, founder of General Motors, having lost his control contrived through his new company, the Chevrolet, with the help of the Du Pont millions, to retain the helm. Nash resigned, and Chrysler became general manager of the Buick Company. Nash was planning to take over another automobile company in which he wished Chrysler to join him. Just at this time Durant offered Chrysler the presidency of the Buick Company at a salary of $75,000 per year. He informed Durant that he had other plans under consideration. He was given thirty days to consider the offer. As the other plans did not materialize, Chrysler accepted a contract for three years and became president of the Buick Company at the salary mentioned, which was eventually to reach $500,000 a year. He stipulated, however, on taking the job, that he must have full authority, subject only to Durant, for whom he had great respect. Despite their mutual confidence, it was Durant's persistent interference with factory operations that eventually terminated the business relationship and led to Chrysler's leaving the Buick company.

Upon the termination of Chrysler's service, the company gave him the opportunity of purchasing a very large amount of the "employee stock." As this required a greater cash investment than was then convenient, the company further agreed to loan him, on his shares, the purchase price of some $15 per share, and also to purchase the shares back, on his demand, at $30 per share.

These papers, drawn in a rather diffuse and technical form, Chrysler carried in his pocket, not realizing that he had a sizeable fortune within reach. As he was about to sail for Europe, he thought he should discuss the matter with his old friend, Billy Durant (no longer with the General Motors Company) who sent him to me. It was then that he learned of the real import of his papers, which he said he had never fully understood. He said that he knew he was entitled to something, but he did not know how much or just how to go about getting it. He directed me to proceed with the matter in my own way, giving me a simple power of attorney to this effect.

Several written demands were promptly made on his behalf by me: first, that the company deliver to him,

at the cost price of $15 per share, the prescribed num-
ber of shares at a stated bank; second, that the company advance to him, at that time and place, the purchase price of $15 per share, to pay for the shares;
finally, that the company repurchase the shares at the
agreed price of $30 per share, recouping itself for the
amount of the loan. These demands delivered all together seemed to create some consternation among the
General Motors officials. It was first suggested that the
contracts were *ultra vires* and hence unenforceable.
Then, from all sides, efforts were made to dissuade me
from pressing the demands. It was finally stated that
the company would vigorously resist them as *ultra
vires*. Undaunted, and confident that the claims were
both legal and equitable, I proceeded, and ere long
I collected the full demand in cash. When Chrysler
was informed by cable of the recovery, he considered
it truly miraculous, and often thereafter spoke of it
as a remarkable achievement. In fact, it was essentially
the simplest kind of situation.

When Chrysler was questioned by me as to how he
earned his large Buick salary, he replied that when he
took the job, the company was making more than thirty
millions. After the satisfaction of his claim, he frequently discussed his later activities with me, toward
whom his personal gratitude never lessened. He always
wished me to participate in his new ventures.

He had hardly left the Buick company when he was snapped up by John N. Willys, originally a bicycle dealer in Elmira, New York, who was then going into automobile manufacturing on a large scale. Walter Chrysler, whose name was already magical in the industry, was hired at a salary reputed to be one million dollars a year, but before he could collect his full salary the concern foundered. Again he was in the market for a job. The A. N. Brady estate and its banking affiliates at that time had a very considerable investment in the Maxwell Motors Company, which developed out of the original U. S. Motors Company, after it had failed. The successor, Maxwell Motors, had large plants and equipment, but also large debts, and had not been doing so well. Chrysler was induced to assume its management by the offer of a salary, stock bonus, profit participation, and stock options. Again Walter Chrysler went to work. The whole aspect became different. It did not take him long to change the color of the Maxwell figure from red to black. He embarked on a career of enlarging and diversifying its products.

As he saw his possibilities, he was no longer happy in working under an unsuccessful name, and the company name was changed to Chrysler. This was the birth of the great Chrysler company. Chrysler rapidly acquired other important companies, and finally took over the Dodge company at an unprecedented price. The Chrysler company was now in the front rank, and its shares soared as its business boomed. Walter Chrysler was conceded a giant in the industry. The former Buick employee had become a formidable competitor, costing General Motors many times what it had paid him on the cancellation of his contract. He was soon regarded as the ablest automotive expert in the country, and his merchandising methods kept pace with his products. His engines were the most effective; his designs the latest; his cars, cabs, busses, and trucks, of every type, waged a strong competition for the nation's patronage.

But Walter Chrysler had not changed. He still loved racy stories. He was still the approachable "hail-fellow-well-met" to his old cronies. No detail of automobile manufacture and merchandising was too trivial for his attention. Truly on his own, by reason of his astounding talent and irrepressible ability, he created a giant enterprise which commanded world-wide recognition. His non-egotistical stories of his lifetime activities limned a sharp portrait of the man; his later history, well known to his contemporaries, served to supply some further details, without changing the basic outline of the portrait which he himself had painted.

Walter Chrysler reached his eminence the hard way, by muscle and grime, by industry and study; always self-reliant, he knew his own power, and he did not fear any mechanical job. He was willing to be judged by his results. Never shirking a duty or a task, he fought his way to the top. He ascribed seventy percent of his success to his devoted wife, who stepped down socially when she married him and kept pace with him all the way up the ladder of success. Guided by her judgment, strengthened by her confidence, eager for her approval, he was happy in feeling that he had merited her devotion.

His name has become a symbol in the automobile industry and his great institution has pushed on to greater achievements. In the center of New York City he erected a monumental building, second in size and height only to the Empire State Building, rather as a landmark for his company than for himself. No Horatio Alger legend of "rags to riches" exceeds the story of Walter P. Chrysler. But his fortune was the fruit of his own efforts. Walter Chrysler owed nothing to anyone but himself and to his wife. The institution which he founded and fostered is his true memorial, and the one which above all he would have wished.

In an era of imaginative enterprise, he was one of the foremost participants. In an age of mechanical precision and development, he was second to none. In a period of unprecedented expansion and inflation, he kept his feet steadily on the ground; and as a master of his craft he had no superior. Truly, he was the embodiment of American energy, ambition, and achievement, a leader among the great industrialists. Despite his outstanding ability he was innately a very modest man. He exhibited but few of the trappings of wealth. Always sociable and approachable, there was no trace of conceit or superiority in his make-up. He never assumed to be other than a master mechanic who knew every detail of his trade and whose one ambition was to turn out the very best machine which his brain and his organization could perfect.

He did not need to have recourse to partners, for he could obtain any amount of capital by merely asking for it. He borrowed gigantic sums but never beyond his ability to pay. His associates were his collaborators and his personal friends. Walter Chrysler finished as he began—a master mechanic; one of the greatest automobile geniuses America has ever produced.

Chrysler believed absolutely in those who in the course of his career had proved themselves to him. He was a man of tireless energy, completely satisfied with his single ambition, who grew with his own development. He was a pioneer, always sure of his course and of himself. Despite the millions of dollars which rewarded his efforts and his genius, his sole pride lay in the perfection of that mechanical construction to which he gave his life. His career is a monumental example of what can be achieved by the unswerving devotion to an idea when it is joined with indefatigable energy and the imagination of genius.

JOHN H. PATTERSON
(1844-1922)

One of the most remarkable personalities ever to
appear in our industrial history was John H. Patterson.
When he was humbled by his defeat in the Government suit against him and his associates, he told me, in
the preparation of the appeal, of his early career and
of his arduous effort in building a great enterprise,
which I will endeavor accurately to report.

This future czar of his industry, at the age of twenty-
three, a sandy-haired farm boy, fresh from college, had
no opportunities and apparently no equipment. His first
real job was as toll collector on a canal. As his duties
left him idle time, he also went into the coal and wood
business with his two brothers. His talent for business
was soon revealed even in that modest sphere. He was
known for delivering the cleanest, best merchandise,
and giving the fairest weight. By nature rather careless
about the intake, he acquired a crude machine to reg-

ister his sales. He had seen it at the little barber shop where he went to be shaved. The barber, not being very good at figures, had contrived a crude contraption that, by pressing levers rapidly in succession, would produce numbers which he would then add up. Patterson was intrigued by it.

After he and his brothers had made a little money, they aspired to bigger things. First they considered farming and cattle raising, but soon decided that this held scant opportunity for advancement. He then bethought himself of the machine. What it had done for him it could do for others. It had been made by the National Manufacturing Company of Dayton, Ohio, a concern notoriously unsuccessful. But young Patterson had a vision of its possibilities. He induced his brothers to join him in buying the capital stock from the local owner. Repenting of his bargain the next day, he offered $1,000 forfeit to be relieved of the purchase; but the former owner declined to let him off, saying that he "would not take the stock back as a gift."

The business was obviously to be manufacturing and selling, neither of which John Patterson knew anything about. He was forty-one years old. He had very little money. The company was "down at the heels." It had neither capital nor customers; its factory was a skeleton. But Patterson, beginning from scratch, made up his mind to renovate and reorganize the company from top to bottom. He took immediate charge. He was soon convinced that he could turn out a machine which every thrifty merchant would want, if it only did the work, and was marketed by men who believed in it and knew how to sell it. From this point on, he excluded every other consideration. He saw the whole world in terms of his cash register. How could his machine benefit the merchant? He believed that if he could achieve the benefit he evisaged, he need not worry about the profits. He would produce the best of all possible machines, and, by education, produce the best of all possible salesmen. No matter how high the score, he would never cease to improve it.

For everything he did, he had a practical and definite objective. He might be called quixotic, a crank, a despot, or even a maniac, but he would go ahead undisturbed in his own way as he saw it. With him, his business became as sacred as a religion, admitting of no doubts or skepticism. His motto was: " 'Good enough' is the enemy of progress." It always had to be better. And this was his eternal principle in the factory and in the field. The sole reason which he always gave for whatever he did was: "It pays!"

There was no expedient for the improvement of his product that he ignored. He soon discovered and hired that mechanical genius, C. F. Kettering, who was to become such a potent factor in the automobile industry. From this fertile mind he drained many ideas, devices, and innovations for the improvement of his machine. Providing the most attractive and pleasant working conditions for his help, Patterson admitted that he exacted strict compliance with his arbitrary conditions for their welfare, believing that well-paid, well-fed, well-housed workmen were a good investment. "It pays," he said.

From the start he realized only too well that there was no ready demand for his product. Indeed, he found a stubborn resistance by merchants, and particularly by clerks, who regarded a cash register as a reflection on their integrity. But he was sure that all this could be overcome by graphic demonstrations and by pure arithmetic. To do this, he needed super-salesmen. Convinced that men worked hardest when endeavoring to gain a reward, he invented numberless schemes to spur them by additional compensation. Since the ordinary salesman was not equipped to do justice to his product, he would provide uniform and expert education. His institution became a technical business university. To make sure that his salesmen were properly trained for their work, he prepared a detailed manual or "primer" which told them everything about salesmanship and demonstration. Every man had to learn that "primer" word for word. And

woe to him who was remiss or careless in its use! Thus
he made sure that every salesman would make a similar presentation.

Inside the factory his methods were similar. He
wished for ideas as well as service. Periodic prizes were
given for helpful suggestions, and public recognition
was accorded to prize winners. He kept a careful personal supervision over every department. His commendation would be freely given, yet always as a prod
for still better performance. There is a legend that on
one occasion when a department head reported a record of one hundred percent, Patterson said: "Are
you satisfied?"

"Yes," answered the proud department head.

To this Patterson responded: "All right. You are
fired."

His university turned out many remarkable graduates. Yet when their expertness menaced his authority,
he parted company with them. Many of our present-
day industrial leaders are his graduates.

By reinforcing every feature of his machine, its
production and its marketing, he succeeded in proving
that what was at first looked upon as a "freak" device
was, in fact, an infallible and indispensable book-
keeper; the cheapest and most reliable any merchant
could acquire. It became the friend and often the
saviour of the small businessman. The grocer or the

butcher need no longer conduct his business carelessly. No longer need sales or receipts be matters of guess-work or slovenly accounting. Here was a machine worth its weight in gold. It would itemize and total the sales, furnish the customer with a receipt, flash the amount of his purchase before his eyes, and never make a mistake. It would do everything except buy and sell the merchandise, acting as a mute and infallible monitor. It promoted accuracy as well as honesty. It would relieve the salesman of argument or questioning, protecting him and his employer at the same time. Almost like wildfire it began to sweep the nation, and, before long, the whole world. Each year brought new improvements. Patterson was never satisfied. His high pressure in the factory and in the field was never relaxed.

This remarkable career had been built without outside capital. It rose like the Phoenix from its own ashes. Year by year it grew from its own earnings, although often in the early days on the verge of insolvency. Patterson threw into it everything he had or could get, supremely confident that it would justify the sacrifice, and in this he was never wrong. Extravagant as he was with what he put in, just as careful was he with what he took out. For distribution, as for everything else, he had a set formula. At first two percent, and later not more than six percent was paid for invested capital; one half of the rest must remain in the business as additional working capital, the other half would be proportionately divided among his employees, from the top down to the humblest workman. He himself must be the boss, yet his people must feel that they had a proprietary interest in the business.

He was a man of many idiosyncrasies, in little as well as in big things. He could be lavish, and he could be parsimonious. No employee whom he sent for knew whether he was to be rewarded or reprimanded. Snug contentment was his *bête noire*.

He thought in symbols. Picture illustrations were his obsession. The number five had some cabalistic significance for him. His points were always five in number. His programs always had five headings. He had five major features in all his ideas. He could not talk in conference or in convention without a blackboard or a huge pad on an easel beside him. This went with him to every business interview. With a piece of crayon in his hand, white for the blackboard, red for the pad, he wrote his points and drew his pictures as he spoke. When he left, he would gather up the pad sheets and take them with him.

He was enmeshed in inconsistencies. Inconspicuously dressed in ordinary business attire, he required his salesmen always to look affluent. While he personally never sold any products, he knew and taught more about selling than any man alive. As autocratic as an emperor, as decisive as a general, he was constantly searching for new ideas. Though eager to develop the greatest expertness on the part of his working force, he would tolerate no insubordination, for he abhorred independence which questioned his authority. He himself was a college graduate, yet he had no patience with collegiate education, except that given in his own industrial university. Meticulously watchful of business expenditures, he gave no attention whatever to his own. The principle of accuracy on which he built his machine and his institution he wholly disregarded in his personal private life. In one particular he was invariably consistent. He was as neat a man as ever lived, and he required that everybody and everything about him be scrupulously neat.

With the eye of an artist he was proud of his machine's symmetry, but he took little interest in the fine arts. In an industry full of invention, he was not an inventor. His ideas of health were highly capricious but often fundamentally sound. Trouble he detested, yet one of his favorite aphorisms was: "The price of progress is trouble." Engaged in producing a machine, he experimented not with mechanisms so much as with men. For his people his education was strict but profound. He detested long words, yet no one knew better than he the power of language. Bubbling over with ideas, he was hesitant in speaking. And so this tireless enthusiast with his evangelistic fervor became a human dynamo, which developed a product and a crew that earned an accolade of merit as universal as the word "Sterling."

The National Cash Register not only dominated the field, it defied substantial competition, constantly becoming more firmly entrenched. Many competitors appeared but all seemed to meet an early defeat. Complaints from prostrated rivals, who were the victims of its ruthless competition, began to reach the Department of Justice until finally the Government instituted criminal proceedings against the company, Patterson, and all his top-line associates. They were all indicted in Cincinnati, Ohio. The case created a furor. It seemed to be interminable. After some six months of constant sessions, with reams of testimony, all were found guilty and all but one sentenced to fines and imprisonment. That one was a rather unimportant individual who had been caught up in the dragnet and who had no counsel. When asked what he had to say as to why sentence should not be pronounced on him, he quietly responded that he had done nothing, and that no evidence had been adduced against him. Then started a scurry of court and prosecuting counsel to discover what evidence against him there was in the record. Their search proved to be futile, so the Court set aside the verdict against him, although he was the only one without a personal lawyer.

There was one striking and damaging bit of evidence showing an incident typically Pattersonian. At a National Cash Register convention he made an address on "Competition," drawing on his ever-present blackboard the figure of a dog which he labeled "Competition." He declared that the tail of the dog, "Competition," should be dismembered where he drew a line—across the neck of the dog. This was claimed to demonstrate his attitude toward his competitors. The effect was devastating and most harmful to his case.

Patterson was shattered by the verdict. His heart's treasure had been hurt. The love of his life was traduced. He seemed at his wit's end. Then Providence came to his rescue. The Dayton flood occurred while he was in Dayton with me, working on his appeal, seemingly in despair. At once, with the vigor and celerity which were habitual to him, he turned his entire plant into an improvised hospital and relief station. Boats and rafts were hastily thrown together under his direction. Nurses and hospital aides were recruited from among his employees. Thousands of lives were saved and scores of homeless families were succored and united by his generosity and timely ingenuity. He, his daughter, his son, and his employees were ceaselessly, night and day, making sandwiches, preparing cots and food, directing salvage, caring for the wounded, and housing the helpless victims. There at his blackboard stood Patterson in command, writing his orders as he shouted—so many stretchers to send out, so many boats to be manned, so much food to be prepared, so many quarters to be readied for incoming cases, bulletins to be issued to the press as well as information about the missing.

He was the efficient commander-in-chief who organized his own Red Cross Army, bringing order out of chaos. Overnight he became a national hero, and the National Cash Register Company was hailed nationwide as a philanthropic institution. The hated company became beloved. No longer were they the hardhearted monopolists on which the public wished to wreak vengeance. When the appeal came to be heard, the most effective argument on his behalf was one which was not mentioned—his wonderful relief work in the Dayton flood. It was quite a different man who appeared before that Appeal tribunal. He was no longer the ruthless industrialist pictured by the prosecution. The conviction was duly reversed. Patterson and his associates were cleared.

From his own statements made to me in the preparation of his appeal, certain of his traits clearly emerged. One who listened to his story could not fail to be profoundly impressed by it. Patterson was truly a

captain of industry. Generally referred to as an inventor, he was, in fact, a farsighted master-merchant.
His associates indulged this clear-eyed strong-jawed,
full-mustached *enfant terrible* in his many peculiari-
ties, for they realized that he was without a peer after
his own fashion. He successfully marketed an expensive
machine to the most thrifty merchants throughout the
world by proving that the price was inconsiderable
when compared with the service.

From his forty-first year to his seventy-eighth, his
life was unremittingly devoted to his beloved idol. He
who had been looked upon as a "crack-brain" had
spread his work around the world, winning an unparalleled industrial victory. He had also made countless contributions to the betterment of his fellowmen,
which, though unheralded, demonstrated the sincerity
of his dictum that "Shrouds have no pockets." Here was
a pioneer, truly great in his performance, sincere in his
philanthropy, and unbeatable at his job. Every concern
which today uses a cash register (and many who are
using similar machines evolved from Patterson's ideas)
owes a deep debt of gratitude to that remarkable man.
The indispensable cash register which stands on almost every counter, is itself a veritable monument to
him. The National Cash Register was in truth the
personification of John H. Patterson. It was not only
his dream, it was also his personal achievement. The

men whom he employed drew not only their education but also their inspiration from his personality. Not only did he achieve a financial success, but he also demonstrated the vision, the generalship, and the resourcefulness of an industrial genius. Through him a new mechanical device was given to the world—one that, owing to him, has become an essential in our commercial life. While he did not invent the cash register, it was through him that it was developed, perfected, and made available everywhere.

GEORGE EASTMAN
(1854-1932)

From the panic of 1907 to the depression of 1929, America experienced a magnificent era of development and expansion. That initial seismic shock of the twentieth century tested our moorings to the utmost. Numerous unsound situations were uncovered; widespread damage had to be repaired; many readjustments and protective safeguards had to be instituted. But despite the devastating havoc and the resulting unemployment, the country and its great enterprises emerged stronger and more resplendent than ever. The stimulant of World War I quickened energy, fostered invention, promoted productivity, and brought new leaders to the forefront. Many, who for years had been assiduously working, growing to maturity, came into the public view. Prominent among them was George Eastman, the erstwhile humble bank clerk of Rochester, New York, who brought the wonders of photography into every American metropolis and village.

It was after Eastman found himself defeated in a
disastrous government action against his company as
a monopoly, as the result of which it became the
target for endless triple damage suits, that he at some
length told me, as one of his counsel, of his history,
his ambitions and his activities, all of which were intimately involved in a very serious situation. Neither
egotistical nor given to self-indulgence, he told me a
story which furnished a rare opportunity to understand
the nature and the motives of this most unusual character.

In appearance he was rather slight, of medium stature, with clear-cut, regular features, a high forehead,
and sparse gray hair. He always wore spectacles. Re-
served and quiet in manner and speech, rather old-
fashioned in dress, with none of the trappings of
wealth, with his white lawn tie and round cuffs, he
resembled nothing so much as a sober, dignified country
preacher. He had no personal extravagances, but was
always open-handedly generous. He found his pleasure
in music and art, in his great enterprise, and in his affectionate associates. Those few who believed in him
at the start and who proved their loyalty by their devotion and financial contributions found themselves
richly rewarded by his achievements.

This retiring bachelor was an unobtrusive patron of

education, whose novel enterprise had its roots in the laboratory and the university. Despite his extraordinary commercial and engineering talents, he was at heart a public-spirited American. Starting at the bottom, with his long-range vision and his unrelenting determination, with unshakable confidence in himself and his plans, he made rapid strides, and literally produced a new industry. In his zeal for greater achievements he borrowed notable discoveries from abroad and particularly from the German scientists, which he supplied to the American public, placing them within the range of a modest purse.

He was unique in his work, indefatigable in improvements, and a pioneer far ahead of any in his field. He became an acknowledged leader both in production and in merchandising. Merit and effort raised him to a position beyond reach. He gave us not only a new but also a most valuable instrument. However, the Government looked upon his enterprise as so dominant that it could be regarded as a virtual monopoly. A court judgment for its decimation was obtained. The execution was postponed so that he might furnish many and, indeed, essential optical and photographic instruments vital for World War I. When he undertook to comply with the decree, the court in its wisdom realized that by trimming off a few rough edges the Eastman Company would be benignly shriven and could emerge with judicial blessing. In the wake of the proceedings, competitors swarmed like bees, eager to extract the honey which they thought would be laid open for them by "triple damage" suits. Eastman, never having intended or believed that his activities were offensive, was eager and anxious to make a fair and equitable settlement, with as little disturbance as possible. In a test case he offered a generous payment which was declined, to a litigant who dreamed of a fantastic recovery only to discover, when subjected to judicial scrutiny, that his collectible damages were far less than Eastman's offer. That was the end of the "swarm." Eastman proceeded undisturbed in his great work.

When he came to see me to pay his bill, he stated that a great service had been rendered him and his company for which he was anxious to pay for generously. When he asked me the amount of our bill, I told him that I had found it somewhat difficult to admeasure the correct value of the service that had been rendered. Seeing my hesitancy in stating the fee, Eastman then volunteered that, while he did not wish to appear ungrateful or niggardly, he had taken the liberty of bringing along with him a check for $50,000, and if that were not, in my judgment, sufficient, he would be glad to supplement it by any amount I might suggest. I told him that I thought it most generous and more than I would have asked. Thereupon he stated that it was not more than we had earned and that he gave it with a sense of gratitude that he would never forget. I thanked him heartily; as he left me he said that our generosity had touched him deeply and had pleased him quite as much as the excellent service which had been rendered.

One other serious complication had involved Eastman's company. Through scientific research, his laboratories and engineers perfected a practical sensitive film to supplant the old-style dry plate. Suddenly an obscure minister turned up who had received an early patent involving the same principle. While the Eastman Company's product was far in advance of anything heretofore known and had been evolved from its own learned research and endless experimentation, there was no denial that the basic idea had first been announced by the minister patentee of whom they knew nothing. So a litigation followed. It was ended by the Eastman Company making an adjustment running into millions of dollars. There was nothing in this situation which impugned Eastman personally, or that even suggested that his company had intended to appropriate the idea of another. It was only a technical infringement (as to which there was even some possible doubt); but Eastman wanted no doubt as to his good faith or fair dealing. He preferred to pay. The litigation was a source of keen regret to Eastman, who was always anxious for his great institution to be, like Caesar's wife, beyond reproach. When the immense scope and the infinite variety of his products are considered, it seems almost miraculous that he had so few legal complications.

His researches, his productions of films and materials, his development and simplification of photographic devices, all of amazing efficiency, became the most outstanding of their kind in the world.

His gifts to others far exceeded his own fortune. Although his was the idea, his the inspiration, and his the unremitting industry which created his world-famous enterprise, he generously gave the credit to his able associates, whose services he was disposed to rate higher than his own. He began with a hobby. With his meager funds and at personal sacrifice, he indulged himself in its study and development. He soon began to see visions of its immense possibilities. His hobby became his single interest, stirring his ambition and inspiring him to ever greater heights. Strangely enough, his commercial development kept pace with his scientific progress. What had started almost as an intriguing toy, grew into an essential commodity. While his faithful friends amassed fortunes and rose to positions of honor and influence, he himself kept in the background. The public interest was centered in the product rather than in the man. Everybody came to know the Eastman cameras; few knew anything about George Eastman.

Generally regarded as a typical American industrialist, skilled in the intricacies of big business, he was in no sense a tycoon. He would be more fittingly deemed essentially as a philanthropist, who did his utmost for his countrymen in opening up an undiscovered field, silently departing when he believed his effectiveness over, leaving the memory of a masterful character of whom we are entitled to be proud, with a startling list of charitable donations.

With no urge for public recognition, he had the enduring courage of an evangelist. He developed an unknown territory where there had been no explorer. He developed untraveled commercial fields in which he had to blaze his own trail. Starting with an idea which was truly inspirational, his devotion and his industry, like his confidence, were inexhaustible. By judicious advertising and meticulously careful manufacturing, he carried to the public a message which made good its promise. He inaugurated a system of developing the photographic negative and of printing the image so that the camera owner need only to take a picture. "You push a button—we do the rest," became a world-wide slogan. Seeking a short, catchy name, he conducted a prize contest from which emerged the striking name of "Kodak." The Eastman Kodak became world-famous, as did the popular term, "snapshot."

All this was the highest type of commercial exploitation, constantly reinforced by the merit of his instruments. From the conventional glass dry-plate, itself an advance over the old wet one, he went into "celluloid" films. In due course the Eastman film became standard. By clever devices he did away with the "dark room," enabling the Kodak user, in broad daylight, to withdraw an exposed film and to replace it with fresh sensitive film. Finally his remarkable machine became so simple that any amateur could operate it. No home was without a Kodak. As the motion-picture industry grew, his company produced the rapid, accurate films needed for its use. His concern soon became the chief supplier of the negative and positive stock for motion-picture producers. Thus, in retrospect, we may see the gradual development from a photographic dry-plate, old-style clumsy box on a tripod to the small, simple, quick-acting, one-hand machine with which a child can do what formerly could be done only by an expert; indeed, can do it even better. The history of that development is the life of George Eastman.

The service he has rendered to the public far exceeds the munificent charities which mark his career. And, through it all, George Eastman, the inventor, the industrialist, the benefactor, and the public-spirited citizen, was ever the same unassuming gentleman as when he started at the bottom. The glory and the fame of his product have tended to obscure the virtues and the talents of the man. But for imagination, ability, and devotion to a great idea, he has few peers in our history of industrial achievement. Those few who knew him well feel that they enjoyed a high privilege. Modern photography, both applied and scientific, owes him a far greater debt than is generally realized. His institution is a model for American enterprise; he himself is an exemplar for every ambitious American industrialist, his generosity needs no elucidation.

He was one of the first to make his employees his partners. His outstanding trait was his willingness, indeed his eagerness, to share the fruit of his work with his associates. He brought to the world one of the essentials of the way of life. Its benefits are not to be measured by the financial returns to him, his associates, or to his company. Indeed, it would be hard to conceive a world today deprived of the great blessings of photography which George Eastman made accessible to the humblest individual. He was not only a great pioneer, an expert manufacturer, and a farsighted merchant, but essentially a true benefactor to mankind.

Eastman's most striking trait was his extreme modesty. He never courted honor or distinction. Entitled as he was to the highest recognition of scientific institutions, he did not believe that his scientific achievements justified it. He looked upon himself merely as a workman sincerely devoted to his craft. He meant to turn out a finer photographic machine than had ever been devised. Though the world beat out and trampled a path to his door, it did not influence his estimation of himself. Still, no man was ever prouder of his handiwork than was George Eastman. It was his life and his love; outside of it, he had no other. Instinctively, he believed that his work in popularizing photography would prove a real boon to society, not only for its amusement, but also for its daily requirement. While he did not disdain to reap substantial profits from his enterprise, he never failed to appreciate the responsibility which these profits entailed. He believed that a workman was worthy of his hire; but he also believed that it was a workman's duty to perfect his product and to make his labors beneficial to his fellowmen.

George Eastman was never envious nor covetous, but in his own industry his aspirations were limitless. His contribution to society far exceeds even his great generosity and his sincere devotion to his gifted co-workers. Although photography itself was not his invention, to him we owe, in a large degree, its present general application and its cardinal position in our world of today.

LEONOR F. LOREE
(1858-1940)

Leonor F. Loree was a rugged individualist, who, starting modestly in the world of railroading, became the conceded dean of railroad systems in the United States—and in almost every capacity. He had grown up with the industry. He knew everything about it, from the building of locomotives, boxcars, and passenger cars, the laying out of routes, and the maintenance of operation and road beds, to the forming of a vast continental system. He was the doctor who was called in when a railroad was *in extremis,* and his patients always recovered. He was a devout believer in the "iron horse," undisturbed by the menace of other means of transportation such as busses and airplanes. He fashioned his own boxcars in order to reduce the number of parts. On the occasion of his projected deal with the Pennsylvania Railroad, he discussed with me some phases of his personal history and

outlined his views as to railroading as well as his
matured ideas for the treatment of railroad systems.
These outlines and the personality of the man behind
them made a fascinating story.

His goal was the harnessing of regional systems, serving and spanning the United States, so as to achieve
the maximum of economy and service with a minimum
of cost and waste. He had his own ideas of management. On his board he had little use for stockholders
as such. He desired able bankers for financial advice,
learned lawyers to avoid pitfalls and to observe the
complicated laws, and experienced operators to attend
to the difficult business of running his roads. He used
to say that he was hired for his expert ability, not for
the securities he might have in his safe-deposit box.

This upstanding citizen was a Spartan for courage.
While he never sought a fight, he never dodged one.
Whether it might be the Interstate Commerce Commission, the Federal Trade Commission, a public service
commission, or a congressional committee, he was ready
to meet them on any issue they might choose, and he
needed neither preparation nor help. Though he was
always responsive to loyal cooperation and invariably
considerate of his associates, he would not tolerate insubordination. When he discovered that an associate
was disposed to give more attention to his personal affairs than to his work, he parted company with him,

regardless of the value of his services. Positive in his views, sure of his facts, he was fearless in promulgating his opinions about matters in his field.

My first contact with Loree was as an adversary in an important litigation in 1913. More than half a century ago, the Delaware and Hudson Company, of which he was now the president, had taken a long-term lease on a large coal property in Pennsylvania, under which that company had agreed to a royalty on all the extracted coal which would pass over a one-inch mesh, with a stipulated minimum yearly payment. In the progress of the industry, large-sized coal became no longer so marketable; consequently, the company proceeded to break down its mined coal, so that very little, if any, would pass over a one-inch mesh. The minimum royalty had become inadequate to enable the owner to pay taxes on the property.

The owners sought some redress from the Delaware and Hudson Company. When this was brought to the attention of Loree, his counsel advised him that his company had no liability. It was an essentially difficult case, since the owners were required to prove the amount of coal as it lay in the veins and to establish the diminution in the royalties to its being broken down to such a degree that the major portion went through a one-inch mesh instead of passing over it, as was originally intended.

Thereupon our firm instituted a suit against this company for an accounting, disputing the right to diminish the royalty by breaking down the coal. After a few years of the most difficult investigation and computation, we succeeded, not only in voiding the lease and recovering the entire minimum but also in securing an accounting for substantial damages, due to this breaking down. All of this was settled by the Delaware and Hudson Company's turning over to the owners the entire mine with all its equipment, machinery, accessories, and appurtenances.

During this protracted lawsuit I had never met Loree, but evidently he decided that in his next serious controversy he would enlist my services. Some years later, Loree invited me to visit him in his apartment. He then told me a remarkable story, and asked me to take the matter in hand. He later told me that he had conferred with his son, a vice-president of the Guaranty Trust Company, who advised him to seek the assistance of those lawyers who had beaten him in the coal lawsuit.

He said when the policy of transcontinental systems was sponsored by the Government, an alliance was formed by him with General Atterbury, head of the Pennsylvania system, to acquire the control of the Lehigh and Wabash shares in the open market for the plan for a national system. Loree was to contribute shares of his Delaware and Hudson Company, and the Pennsylvania, a corresponding amount in cash, with which their banker, Otto H. Kahn, was to buy Lehigh and Wabash shares in the open market for the joint account of the Pennsylvania, and the Delaware and Hudson Company. All this was reduced to an informal memorandum, initialed by all three. The operation proceeded until Loree learned that the banker had turned over all the purchase shares to the Pennsylvania company, offering to return the Delaware and Hudson shares to Loree.

Then, undismayed by the stature of his opponents, Loree, on my advice, went after the banker and the Pennsylvania so forthrightly, that he collected in cash the full amount of which he claimed his company was deprived. These funds he invested in his company's portfolio and in due course purchased various prime securities for his company.

The depression of 1929 decreased their value considerably. One day, when in consultation on another matter, I asked him why he did not distribute those funds to his stockholders to handle for themselves, rather than to allow them to depreciate in his treasury. "No," he replied, "I shall use them some time to buy a railroad."

"What railroad would you buy?" I asked.

"I have not quite decided," he replied, "but I think

the New York Central would by far suit me best."

"When do you think its shares will be cheaper than now?" was the next question, to which he replied: "Probably never."

The market price then was about $13 a share. "Why not proceed now to buy them?" I asked.

Without a moment's hesitation he said: "Right! Go and make the arrangements to buy up 10% of the issued shares of the New York Central, which I understand is the limit possible without application to the Public Service Commission."

I then visited the New York Central bankers, Messrs. J. P. Morgan and Company, and asked one of the heads of that firm who was well known to me: "How do you intend to support the New York Central shares?"

The answer was: "I do not know how, and I can see no immediate support for them." Then I asked whether he would like an open order to purchase up to 10% of the New York Central stock.

To this he promptly replied: "There is only one person who could give us such an order, and his name is Leonor F. Loree!"

"Correct," I assented. "What is necessary to be done before you can accept the order which Loree is prepared to give you?"

The banker said that there should first be a confer-

ence with the heads of the New York Central—which
was arranged immediately. At that meeting Loree
was asked only one question by the chairman, Jackson
Reynolds, head of the First National Bank of New
York: "Is this the Pennsylvania who is to be the purchaser?"

Loree, with a smile, answered: "It is not the Pennsylvania, although the money comes from the Pennsylvania. The Delaware and Hudson Railroad Company
will be the actual purchaser." Then he explained the
source of the funds.

This having been found satisfactory, Reynolds suggested that the President of the New York Central,
Fred E. Williamson, should be consulted. When Williamson was summoned and informed of the suggestion, he said: "I acquired my railroad schooling
under Mr. Loree. There is no one for whom I have
a higher respect and regard. I should be delighted to
have him in our company and on our board. There is
nobody I would rather have." Thereupon the orders
were given, and in due course, Loree's company became
the principal New York Central stockholder. He served
on its board as long as he lived. His purchase grew
very profitable for his company and the association
happy for himself and for his New York Central associates.

Loree was always most considerate of his stockholders. He never failed to attend their meetings. No person was too unimportant, no question too trivial for his personal attention. With his tall, portly figure, and his short, shaggy beard and shock of iron-gray hair, he looked like a benign Job. It was interesting to watch him bustling about, he himself serving sandwiches, coffee, and cakes to the elderly ladies who were present year after year. His manner was always kind and courteous, his speech temperate, and his motives above suspicion. He was direct, blunt, and decisive, but always respected and beloved by his associates.

Loree pursued a very careful procedure for his meetings of stockholders. A stenographer was always present, taking down everything that transpired. The meeting would complete its agenda, then recess for a lunch of sandwiches, coffee, cakes, and ice cream, which the company supplied. Immediately after lunch, the meeting would be resumed. The stenographer would read his typewritten record then and there, to be approved by the stockholders with such changes as they might prescribe. Consequently, there could never arise any question as to what had been done at these meetings.

Although much of his life was spent in the atmosphere of financiers and politicians, Loree never stepped out of his role as a practical railroader: his personal inspection trips covered every inch of his lines, no detail of operation escaping his scrutiny. The stock market

had no lure for him. He was never interested in speculation. He was always keenly alive to new conditions
and endowed with the resourcefulness to handle them.
A born leader, an accomplished specialist, and a patriotic American, he will always be revered by those who
knew him, and an example for those who may study his
work. He was one of the last of those dauntless pioneers
who braved so much and worked so diligently to bring
us to where we are today.

As an executive, Lorce was as able as he was expert
in his field. His sole pride lay in his management. He
asked no acclaim; he sought no special credit or bonus.
With him, his work was his duty, and that duty was
ever his foremost consideration. His well-being consisted not in personal wealth but in the intense gratification of successful performance.

Devoid of ostentation or vanity, giving endless
attention to the details of his great industry, he
never ceased to learn and to progress. For railroading
he had not only devotion, but deep-rooted respect. He
studied and understood its serious responsibilities toward the public. His ambition was not only to make
his company successful operating agencies, but to
justify the confidence that the public as well as his
shareholders reposed in him. He felt himself to be a
public servant, and to him the public service was a
high trust which he discharged to the limit of his great

abilities. Service was his watchword. He believed that
every honest servant should give of his best, for which
no special reward was due.

Loree was in truth a patriarch of the old school, one
whose foresight, diligence, and devotion had developed
America. The proudest guerdon which could have been
rewarded to him, the highest tribute which his stockholders and his public patrons could pay him, was that
he had seen his obligation and had performed it faithfully, with honor and with justified price.

He fraternized with all his people, from the lowliest
to the highest; no work was beneath his dignity; no
detail was too trivial for his personal consideration.
There was no railroad official in the United States who
was not his friend and his personal admirer. Despite
his towering position in the railroad world, no man
was more humble and cooperative in any movement
which was honestly designed to improve and to perfect
the vast railroad systems which spanned the country.
There had been many great railroad men, some more
domineering, more acquisitive, and more despotic, but
none more conscientious or more generally beloved or
more respected than Leonor F. Loree.

WILLIAM C. DURANT
(1861-1947)

No story of the automobile industry would be complete which omits the career of William C. Durant. With his organizing and executive genius, he carved out two gigantic careers, and created one of the nation's greatest institutions, but wrecked himself in the process because of the lure of Wall Street. Beginning as a young insurance man in Flint, Michigan, he borrowed $2,000 to go into the buggy business, selling to a friend one-half share for $1,000. Before he was forty years of age, he was a millionaire. As a buggy manufacturer, he early foresaw the future of automobiles, just as did Henry Ford, and not much later than Ford. Whereas Ford had only a low-priced car in mind, Durant would include all grades and prices. By a series of skillful and daring maneuvers, and a compelling personal charm which was irresistible, he organized a great new company and found very substantial backing for it. On his working staff he enlisted a remarkable group of able men, many of whom are today still in the forefront of the automobile world.

Durant was a soft-spoken man, fertile in ideas, sound in vision, untiring in effort, and resourceful in executive management. His associates became his affectionate friends. The various concerns in related manufacturing, which he acquired for the company, such as the "Delco," the Hyatt Roller Bearing Company, and the Fisher Brothers Body Company, have turned out to be among its greatest assets.

Durant had one serious weakness. As he watched the meteoric rise of General Motors shares and the unprecedented success of its very nature, he could not refrain from participating on the stock market side. He developed into a gigantic market operator. However thriving his company, his market operations became his chief concern. He was sure that the market could go only one way—"up." The inevitable came to pass. Durant found himelf hopelessly involved in a morass of falling values. He was obliged to part with his precious shares and to turn over the management to the more conservative executives who would attend exclusively to its business.

But Durant, though "down" was by no means "out." It took years of planning, careful conservation, and the loyalty of old friends to recoup. Through a new company—the Chevrolet—he acquired control of General Motors, and in September, 1915, he again became the head of that great institution. Then it seemed as though he had the "Midas" touch.

Unfortunately, he had not been cured. The old malady reappeared. He was still intrigued by the market, and almost before he could realize it he was again sucked into that maelstrom. He had built his private fortune up to more than one hundred million dollars. He was carrying some five millions of General Motors shares, but they were all in equities and the menacing debts were stupendous. His fortune evaporated almost overnight. Again he was obliged to step out. The Du Pont Securities Company took over his shares at a price which left him little or nothing. Durant departed, never to return. While he still had many staunch friends in the company and outside it who frequently came to his assistance, despite his brave attempts to organize new automobile companies on his own, he found himself no longer a factor in the industry.

For a while it looked as though Durant would stage a third "comeback" through a new company which he formed to manufacture a cheap car. He told me that his personal accounts with the General Motors Company had never been closed, and that he believed that the company still owed him a substantial sum.

Much as he needed the money, his pride would not allow him to assert a claim. My opinion was that his successors in authority were gentlemen of high honor, unwilling to do him any injustice. After some discussion, he gave his consent for the matter to be brought to the attention of the company's executives. When I did this, they promptly instituted a thorough, accurate audit, and quite voluntarily paid over to Durant the substantial amount to which he was found to be entitled.

He then established the Durant Company, to operate at Flint, Michigan, which had been the principal locale of his former operations. By an intensive selling campaign he sold to the public millions of shares in his company; but his program broke down, and he was faced with a very serious legal situation because of the wide distribution of the shares through salesmen who were none too careful about their promises and representations. It was Fred Fisher, the head of Fisher Brothers, whose company Durant had taken into General Motors, that came to his rescue and saved him from disaster. Meanwhile, a monster factory at Elizabeth, New Jersey, belonging to the crippled Willys Company, was put up for auction. Walter Chrysler turned up as a bidder against Durant, but Durant bid the higher price of some five million dollars and bought the plant. It was the nature of the man to do everything on a gigantic scale; he might fail, but it would not be for lack of daring courage. Even in defeat, his courage and his optimism never left him.

But his magic touch was gone. He was left behind in the stirring march of the industry. His fabulous fortune lost, there remained only the comparatively few General Motor shares which in his heyday he had fortunately set aside in trust for the members of his family and himself. A great leader had finished his job. His day was over; but his work has lived and is today a magnificent tribute to his wonderful talents. His former employee, Walter Chrysler, has publicly paid him many high tributes.

Though Durant had started as a small buggy builder, he became one of the world's greatest automobile manufacturers. He was familiar with each detail of construction, never ceasing to study every possible improvement in that field. He was an accomplished engineer who made a life study of practical engineering as applied to automobiles. He was, likewise, an accomplished financier, as well as an expert on costs. He was always a close student of every development in his industry, and very early in his career he conceived the practical possibilities of his dreams.

Untiring in his own work, he was a hard taskmaster. A keen student of human nature, an unerring judge of

human talent, he became highly expert in every detail
of manufacturing, mechanics, engineering, and merchandising. He was highly adept in public relations,
always sensitive to the public reaction toward the
machines which he turned out; a pioneer in the details
of salesmanship, and in the promotion of the public
esteem for his products. His great fault, if it be a fault,
was interfering with the expert staff, each of whom
was "tops" in his field. It was this propensity which,
as has been shown, led to the greatest loss which his
company sustained—the loss of Walter Chrysler. Except for Chrysler, all of his staff had the highest regard
for his detailed practical knowledge, for his unerring
business judgment, and for his inspiring leadership.
Chrysler's success was due to his being a great mechanic; Durant's because he was a great executive.

Critical as his associates may have been of his market
operations, he was an ardent believer in America, but
a hopeless optimist, who, in his bright dreams, could
see no dull spots. The thousands of General Motors
stockholders, the army of General Motors workmen,
the scores of related enterprises which it supports, are
not only beholden to his superb organization, but also
to that brilliant industrialist who brought it into being,
and who, when he served it, served it well.

Whatever may have been his idiosyncrasies, his
achievements tower so high above them that they are

no longer significant, save to indicate the suffering and disappointment to which they subjected him, despite his monumental and well-nigh incredible accomplishments.

Durant was one of the first to conceive the unlimited possibilites of the automobile industry. He personally chose and assembled the basic constituents for the gigantic enterprise born of his mind. He selected those brilliant executives who, under his leadership, were to bring it to high efficiency. He enlisted the all-important capital and laid out the corporate structure; and in the early days, when the industry was new and the methods untried, it was he who wisely chartered out its course and steered it safely through the storms and stresses which confront every great innovation. Many of the problems which he solved have stood the severe tests of time and keen competition. Every adjunct which he annexed to his major operation has proven highly beneficial. Indeed, it would be difficult to find a single individual whom he chose for his army of co-workers who has not achieved an outstanding career. These are the attributes of greatness; these are the qualities which make a leader. And so, in an impartial retrospect of the industry, no fair estimate can fail to justify Chrysler's characterization that Durant, in some ways, "has been its greatest man."

Durant was truly one of the pioneers in the building of the great American corporations. He it was who laid the solid foundation on which the present greatest American enterprise, the General Motors Company, was built. Moreover, his plans went much further than merely laying the foundation. He conceived, in a large degree, the gigantic structure which has risen from that massive foundation. He sensed the tremendous growth which had begun to be demonstrated by the great Ford Company.

Long before most of the world realized the future developments with automotive machines, Durant visualized their ultimate general use. Moreover, he also foresaw many other contrivances, in the way of machinery, with the growth of the automobile industry; and so at the same time he laid the foundation for these developments and for their many related enterprises.

One cannot fairly appreciate the genius of Durant without realizing that he not only built one of the greatest manufacturing institutions in the world, but that he also assembled a corps of leaders, touched with genius, who put his grandiose ideas into effect, and who were capable, as they have proved, of realizing that which for Durant, had been really only a dream.

Whatever fault might be found with his stock operations and the vicissitudes of his career for which he was alone responsible, credit cannot be fairly withheld from him for the wonderful institution which he translated from an idea to reality. He foresaw the unlimited possibilities in a particular industry just as Columbus disclosed the potential of a New World. The final dark days of both of these dauntless venturers cannot detract from the scope of their imagination nor from the immensity of their dreams.

THE GUGGENHEIMS
Meyer (1828-1905)
Isaac (1854-1922)
Daniel (1856-1930)
Murry (1858-1939)
Solomon R. (1861-1949)
Benjamin (1865-1912)
Simon (1867-1941)
William (1868-1941)

The Guggenheim story is an American epic. On the occasion when the five brothers were sued by their younger brother William, each in his own way told me the family story for the preparation of their defense. This is not the story of one man, but of a family, which owed its strength as well as its success to the precepts of its founder. Its origin was in the younger Meyer Guggenheim, father of the famous brothers.

In 1847, Meyer Guggenheim came to this country with his father, a widower, from Switzerland. On the same ship was a widow, Mrs. Meyers, who was traveling with her daughter, Babette. The elder Guggenheim married the widow; Meyer married Babette. The young couple settled in Philadelphia, and there raised a family consisting of three daughters and eight sons.

Meyer, with his keen commercial sense and his indomitable industry, began business with a horse and wagon as an itinerant merchant, thereby saving overhead expenses and extending his clientele over a large area. He bought his merchandise in the city and sold it in the country. He was a serious reader, especially fond of history. He saw the advantages of education, and was resolved not only to give his children these advantages but also to improve himself. As his business thrived he went into other lines. First he manufactured and sold stove polish, and his eldest son, Isaac, became his traveling salesman. Then he went into the production and sale of lye. In this business he became so successful that the Pennsylvania Salt Company bought him out at a good price. By that time, he had accumulated a comfortable competence which in those days was a fortune. Now he was truly a capitalist.

He engaged in several new businesses as possible openings for his boys. But his principal business was in laces and embroideries. His son, Isaac, took his fourth son, Solomon R., to Europe to place him in charge of a factory at St. Gall, Switzerland. S. R., as he was called, later opened another factory at Plauen, Saxony. The three elder boys attended to the American end of the business. It was in this business that these four had their commercial education.

As a capitalist, Meyer was always aware of promising prospects. A friend in Philadelphia, Mr. Graham, in the grocery business, who had been a good customer for Meyer's lye, offered him a participation in a lead mine, the "A. Y. and Minnie," at Leadville, Colorado. Graham owned a half interest in the mine. He sold Meyer one half of his half—a quarter interest. The other half interest in the mine was owned by Thomas Weir, who was the manager in charge of operations.

Meyer, who knew nothing about mining, decided to look over the property. The country was still wild and unsettled. There he found that operations were not very successful, and that the manager was pessimistic as to the future. As Meyer noted that all about the mine there were other operations apparently profitable, he concluded that this, too, could be made profitable. Without any expert advice he offered to buy the manager's half interest for $50,000. The offer was not immediately accepted, but before Meyer left he made the purchase. Then he asked his lawyer, Mr. Thomas, later United States senator from Colorado, to find a capable manager. Charles Hill was employed, who promptly changed the operation and opened up valuable silver and lead deposits. The "A. Y. and Minnie" mine began to make millions of dollars and continued to do so increasingly.

When Meyer returned to Philadelphia, he told his partner, Graham, what he had done, and he offered him, at cost, one half of his purchase, agreeing to carry it for him. Thus Graham and Meyer became equal partners. The mine continued to make money, and for many years produced large profits for its owners.

Meyer's study of the mining business convinced him that while mining was hazardous, the smelting of ore was not. After the prospectors and the miners took all the risks and produced the ore, the smelter got their business, and at a good profit. Meyer bought an interest in a smelter in which the banking firm of Kountze Brothers of New York was the principal owner. This venture prospered so well that the Kountzes bought out Meyer at a good profit to him. Meyer was again a capitalist.

Convinced that smelting was the safest and most profitable end of mining, he determined to put his boys in that business. S. R. was directed to close out the factories at St. Gall and at Plauen. Though but a youngster, he sold the business and the real estate to advantage, but not until he had arranged for every employee to be retained by the purchasers.

Then Meyer's plan was to build a smelter of his own in the West. Out of loyalty to their home town, it was called the "Philadelphia Smelter." Now the Guggenheim boys were set in the smelting business. In the year 1885, a partnership agreement was made between the four eldest boys, in which Isaac and Daniel put in $50,000 each and S. R. and Murry $15,000 each. As the younger boys, Simon, Benjamin, and William came along (Robert having died), each was to be taken in with equal interest, without any capital contribution. It was on this condition that the father soon turned over to his boys his fortune in the business, receiving only a moderate income to cover his living expenses.

The firm of M. Guggenheim Sons grew rapidly. Each of the sons had his work laid out, and each was kept on his toes. By 1900, the company had become a formidable rival of the great American Smelting and Refining Company, the foremost concern in the American smelting world. This company offered to purchase with its shares of stock the smelting business of M. Guggenheim Sons. Some of the brothers apposed the sale, but the judgment of Daniel, then at the helm, prevailed, and, acting as a unit which was their invariable practice, the sale was made. Thus the seven Guggenheim brothers acquired a controlling interest in the shares of the American Smelting and Refining Company. They at once took charge of it. The youngsters,

Benjamin and William, feeling overshadowed by their five older brothers, took up their shares and went off on their own. The other five, Isaac, Daniel, Murry, S. R., and Simon, remained together and preserved their close association as long as they lived, except for the leave of absence given to Simon for his term as United States senator from Colorado.

The firm continued in the mining business first under the old name of M. Guggenheim Sons and later as Guggenheim Brothers. All have now passed on. S. R., the sage octogenarian, was long the sole surviving partner, who, in conjunction with his brothers' estates, administered such Guggenheim interests as had not been merged into publicly owned corporations. A seasoned veteran in experience and in courage, he always carried high the family banner, upholding the Guggenheim tradition, and proved himself to be a worthy standard bearer and a consistent exponent of the ideals for which that name is respected the world over. His affectionate reverence for his father in no sense lessened with the years. His father was ever his inspiration and his guiding star, to whom he often liked to refer.

All the Guggenheim brothers were great figures; Daniel was the farsighted architect who conceived and laid out the plans, a genius with creative vision and unfaltering courage, the ablest of all the brothers; Murry attended to copper sales and the business de-

tails with outstanding ability as a brilliant merchant;
S. R. went out into the field to make the arrangements
necessary for effectuating the plans and for building
the plants, whose sound independent business judgment always gave his brothers something to think about,
for he was the brother with strong, well-founded convictions who always had to be won over; and Senator
Simon Guggenheim, as a dauntless executive, intelli-
gently administered every enterprise placed in his
charge, particularly the Smelting Company.

The brothers had one unswerving principle: they
always acted as a unit in their business. However they
might disagree among themselves, their differences
were always reconciled. First as smelters and refiners,
then as mine developers, pioneers, and operators, they
made an almost incredible success of whatever they
undertook. They were seldom misled themselves, and
they never consciously misled their friends. In one
notable instance, the Nipissing Mine, in Canada, after
they had paid a large sum for an option to be credited
on the purchase price if the option were exercised, they
found that many of their friends had followed their
lead by investing in the shares. Upon closer investigation they concluded that they had made a mistake, and
they not only forfeited their payments, but took over
all the shares of friends whom they thought had been
misled by their mistake.

When Benjamin was lost in the *Titanic* disaster of April 14, 1912, his five brothers found that his personal business affairs were not in good shape. They promptly came to the rescue and salvaged a comfortable fortune for his widow and daughters. Despite the fact that they had a serious and painful controversy with their youngest brother, William, who sued them for ten million dollars, which was generously adjusted later, when his fortune vanished, his five brothers voluntarily created a million-dollar trust fund for him, which assured his peace of mind and comfort as long as he lived. They felt that they were doing only what their father would have them do.

The Guggenheim mining enterprises almost circled the globe. A curious instance in their history shows the fallibility of human nature. The firm, through the Morgan banking house, had negotiated the sale of a controlling interest (two million shares) in the Chile Copper Company to the great Anaconda Copper Company. The terms were cash or certified check on the delivery of the shares. The agreement of sale, drawn by me, was most unusual. It provided that if for any reason either buyer or sellers failed to go through with the deal, there should be no legal liability; for the Anaconda was a large publicly-owned company while the Guggenheims were a firm. In case of litigation or legal obstruction, the Anaconda Company might find itself

obstructed, but neither party wished the Guggenheim
shares to be tied up or impounded. Each was quite
satisfied to rely on the good faith of the other, despite
the huge amounts involved. It was really only "a gentleman's agreement."

When the day of closing came, the National City
Bank was prepared to pay over the purchase price of
seventy million dollars. The day before the closing,
the bank's president told me that this huge payment
would be made by check of the National City Company
on the National City Bank. He explained that while
the money was on deposit at his bank, certification
would seriously disarrange its clearance and would
subject them to great inconvenience. Though anxious
to be accomodating, I was obliged to decline to waive
the certification. On the day of closing, the bank president appeared at Morgan's with the check for seventy
million dollars, across the face of which was stamped,
as is usual with certified checks, the word "Accepted"
(meaning certified), beneath which was a blank dotted
line for the personal signature of the bank's cashier,
without which the certification would be invalid.
In the intense excitement of the moment, none of
the lawyers, the bankers, the principals, not even
the bank president himself, noticed that the certification was meaningless, as it bore no written signature on the dotted line, and that the check was also

undated. However, the check went through as per schedule, and no one suffered any harm or delay, and it was duly paid in regular course.

This same Chile Copper enterprise was the occasion of an outstanding incident of the Guggenheim ethics. The property had been brought to them by Albert C. Burrage, of Boston, Massachusetts, who had an option for its purchase. In consideration of his transfer of the option to the Guggenheims, and especially of a method for the recovery of the ore, he was to have a very substantial participation. But the Burrage method of recovery proved ineffective. The firm was not prepared to go ahead and before they had discovered a process by which the upper ore could be successfully recovered, the Burrage option expired; what they had received from Burrage had proven to be of no advantage. The Guggenheims then had nothing. When they determined to buy the property and had developed their own successful method for treating the ore by their great engineer, E. A. Capellen-Smith, they had to make a new deal with the owners of the mine. Burrage was not the original sponsor of the property to them. They had previously examined it through their own engineer, Pope Yeatman, and had declined it years before. It was only because Burrage thought he had a successful extracting process, that he had enlisted their interest. Despite disappointment and the possibility that Burrage's rights to participation had lapsed, they reinstated their rights in full and accorded him his entire share proportionately in the sale to Anaconda.

The sons of Meyer Guggenheim fulfilled their father's hope to the utmost. They proved loyal to their tradition, to which they attributed their achievements, of diligence, devotion, and courage. Their growth had been the growth of their industry. Having opened up vast resources of wealth for the benefit of the world, their fortunes had been fairly earned by the benefits they had brought to the public whom they had faithfully and scrupulously served. Of them it may be truly said that they had been not mere "captains" but "generals" of their industry.

These distinguished men, to whom their country had been so bountiful, were not remiss in sharing their good fortunes with their fellow men. Daniel Guggenheim established an aviation fund for a number of leading colleges for buildings and research in aviation. This had done much to advance the science of aviation. With his wife, he endowed the free summer concerts given in Central Park.

Murry Guggenheim, deeply concerned for the physical well-being of the children of New York City, created a most affective dental foundation for their benefit, which is rendering a fine much-needed service to the community.

Simon Guggenheim, in memory of his son, John S. Guggenheim, established a splendid educational foundation for the encouragement of students of science, literature, and the arts, which has awarded and is regularly awarding a multitude of fellowships to deserving aspirants.

S. R. Guggenheim, intensely interested in the progress and development of art, has created an art foundation, especially designed to exhibit, encourage, and patronize the latest type of art production, known as "non-objective art" which has been making astonishing strides in art interest here and abroad.

So each, in his own way, had gladly and generously given to the public a substantial participation in the fruits of his efforts.

Thus the Guggenheim story illustrates the famous anecdote about Meyer, the father of the brothers, who is said to have taken a bunch of faggots and to have shown his sons that as a bunch they could not be broken, but if separated into individual pieces, each piece could be easily splintered. "Hence," he said, "so long as you stay together, you cannot be defeated, but if you separate, you will no longer be indestructible." The prophecy in his fable was only too truly demonstrated, on the one hand, by the failure of the two brothers who went off on their own and, on the other, by the unconquerable power and prodigious success of the five who adhered so devotedly to one another, and who carried out the sage precept of their father.

L'ADIEU

"To live in hearts we leave behind
Is not to die!"
—Thomas Campbell

We have tarried a while with a varied group of departed leaders. All were unusual men who played important roles in the drama of their world. As prominent figures, all were active participants in the cavalcade of the first third of this century. Some of them passed in their apogee; others survived their zenith. But each, because of his individual contribution, is worthy of remembrance; some for their lofty examples, others for their unfortunate mistakes. They fill fond pages in our memory book. That their scores were high and their achievements notable may justify their selection from the album of the past.

Since these men are themselves the authority for their stories, this fragmentary record is respectfully submitted. It may serve, even though faintly, as an echo from lips now silent.

Their voices are not from the tomb,
Surcharged with sadness or with gloom;
But still they speak in accents clear,
For those who yet may care to hear.
Theirs is a message noble, high,
That inspiration does not die!

INDEX

A

Date Due